Books have swept me away,
one after the other, this way and that;
I made endless vows according to their lights,
for I believed them.
Annie Dillard

How to Read Slowly

Reading for Comprehension

James W. Sire

Harold Shaw Publishers
Wheaton, Illinois

To my father
who in his eighties
still reads voraciously

The *Wheaton Literary Series*

Copyright © 1978, James W. Sire

ISBN 0-87788-357-2

Cover photo © 1989 Irish Tourist Board

_____

Library of Congress Cataloging-in-Publication Data

Sire, James W.
  How to read slowly: reading for comprehension /
James W. Sire.
      p. cm.—(The Wheaton literary series)
  Reprint. Originally published: Downers Grove,
Ill.: InterVarsity Press, © 1978.
  Bibliography: p.
  Includes index.
  ISBN 0-87788-357-2
  1. Books and reading. 2. Reading comprehension. I. Title. II. Series.
Z1003.S597 1988
428.4'3—dc19   88-11499
                                 CIP

_____

99

10 9 8 7 6 5 4

Preface to the Second Edition

I was delighted when C. Stephen Board, a very long-time friend (every author should have one who is the director of a publishing house), suggested that this book be brought back into print for the third time. InterVarsity Press issued it first in 1978 under the present title and Multnomah Press in 1984 under the title *The Joy of Reading*. Still, the present edition is only the second since all that was changed in the Multnomah publication was the title.

Here I have updated the reading plan in the Appendix, removing books that no longer seem as important as before and added a few titles published since 1978 and a few older ones I have come to appreciate. In my reading I tend to find an author whose work I like and then devour most of what they have written. Recently these authors include Shusaku Endo, Lewis Thomas, Wendell Berry, Gary Snyder, Frederick Buechner, Annie Dillard, Jorge Luis Borges, Stanislaw Lem, and Czeslaw Milosz. And I have also been immersing myself in the Japanese haiku poetry of Matsuo Basho, Taniguchi Buson, Issa and Masaoka Shiki.

I find each of them fascinating for very different reasons. I commend them to anyone who wants not only what my British friends call a good read but an insight into what it means to be human. May this book be a stimulus to read much, much more than this book! You may even read this book fast, if you promise to read all others slowly.

James W. Sire
Downers Grove
August 1988

Acknowledgments

For Pamela McCorduck, "An Introduction to the Humanities with Prof. Polemy." Copyright reprint with permission of *The Chronicle of Higher Education*, February 9. Copyright 1976 by Editorial Projects for Education, Inc.

For William Carlos Williams, "The Red Wheelbarrow." William Carlos Williams, *Collected Poems, Volume I: 1909-1939*. Copyright © 1938 by New Directions Publishing Corporation.

For the epigraph to chapter five. From *A Portrait of the Artist as a Young Man* by James Joyce. Copyright 1916 by B. W. Huebsch. Copyright 1944 by Nora Joyce. Copyright renewed © 1964 by the Estate of James Joyce. All rights reserved. Reprinted by permission of Viking Penguin Inc. Acknowledgment is also due to The Society of Authors as the literary representative of the Estate of James Joyce.

Polonius: *What do you read, my lord?*
Hamlet: *Words, words, words.*
Polonius: *What is the matter, my lord?*
Hamlet: *Between who?*
Polonius: *I mean the matter you read, my lord.*
Hamlet: *Slanders, sir: for the satirical rogue says here that old men have grey beards, that their faces are wrinkled, their eyes purging [discharging] thick amber and plum tree gum and that they have a plentiful lack of wit, together with most weak hams: all which, sir, though I most powerfully and potently believe, yet I hold it not honesty to have it thus set down, for yourself, sir, should be as old as I am, if like a crab you could go backward.*
Polonius [aside]: *Though this be madness, yet there is method in't.*
Shakespeare, Hamlet

Chapter 1
A Method in Our Madness:
An Introduction to Reading with the Mind

My father is a rancher, a retired purebred Hereford breeder to be exact. All his life he has wanted me to take over the small Nebraska ranch I was raised on. Very early he must have known that that wasn't going to work out. I always had my nose in other things—like electronics, ham radio and books.

I remember one summer, home from college and without a job, I went with our family on the annual Hereford Tour. A caravan of fifty cars and a hundred and fifty ranchers trailed its way from ranch to ranch where cattlemen displayed their herds and let their fellow ranchers and potential customers know just how good their cattle were. A lot of pride went into being selected to be a stop on the tour, and our ranch had been selected that year.

But what did I do? I brought along G. G. Simpson's *The Meaning of Evolution,* just published in paperback at the time. While the rest of the family climbed up on wooden fences and watched the parade of fine Hereford stock, I stayed in the car, enraptured by Simpson, underlining the text and putting brackets in the margins.

A couple of summers later while trying to sell "a method of cooking"—Vita Craft's absolutely unpittable-aluminum-last-a-lifetime cookware—I pulled my junk car to the side of the road and read Stephen Crane's *Red Badge of Courage* and Dostoyevsky's *The Idiot.* That same day I twisted the psychological arms of two sweet, young high-school graduates but made no sale. Forsooth! That summer I bought and read more books than I sold cookware. Early on, reading became for me a way of life—joyous, fascinating, refreshing, challenging. It is out of that context that this book comes.

I don't expect any reader to imitate my own lifestyle nor to adopt point for point the precise values that I would at my best affirm. But I do want to announce at the beginning that I love reading and would like to help others love it too —and do it better.

Is This Book for You?
Primarily this book is for Christians. That is not because I think there is a peculiarly Christian way to read. I don't. Rather, reading well is a broadly human craft and can be practiced by any person with basic intelligence. In fact, most of this book should be useful to anyone who wants to learn how to read better. Still, I am most interested in encouraging Christians to think and read well. Christians, of all people, should reflect the mind of their Maker. Learning to read well is a step toward loving God with your mind. It is a leap toward thinking God's thoughts after him.

Since this book is directed toward Christians, I would ask those who do not consider themselves Christians to forgive the apparent oddness of some of what I say. Maybe, if you hear me out, by the end of the book you won't think it quite so odd.

To be specific, then, I have three basic categories of readers in mind. First are Christians who want to learn how to read better. I am thinking here of those of you who have not specifically studied reading in college. Majoring in chemistry, engineering or economics, you have practiced reading but never looked at it as a craft, something that can be isolated, studied and learned. You have wanted to read primarily to *know*. Your goal has been utilitarian. Surely one important function of reading is education, learning something we don't already know. I hope my book will help you learn better. But I would also like to think that you will come to appreciate reading for its own sake, for that will make everything you read a potential joy.

Second are those of you who have studied literature in college and love it so much you will read anything, even a book on how to do better what you can't stop doing anyway. In this sense, perhaps this book will be a refresher course.

Third are those of you who may be a captive audience, this book having been foisted on you by a well-intentioned teacher. From you I beg indulgence and a small act of faith. Maybe this won't be such a bad text after all.

In one sense this book is a sequel to *The Universe Next Door*. In that book I tried to isolate and define the various ways people today view life. The illustrations for this were drawn from various literary and philosophic works. Some have asked me how to read so that the world view of the author becomes obvious. *How to Read Slowly* is a rather long answer to that short question. But the question is an important one and deserves a careful response.

Reading to understand world views is not something one is likely to do naturally. I was not taught to do this until I studied under Professor Donald Clark at the University of Missouri. I wish someone had taught me to do it sooner. In any case, once learned and practiced, it will stick with you and, I trust, become second nature.

Models and Maps

"Every person carries in his head a mental model of the world—a subjective representation of external reality," writes Alvin Toffler in *Future Shock*.[1] This mental model is, he says, like a giant filing cabinet. It contains a slot for every item of information coming to us.[2] It organizes our knowledge and gives us a place from which to argue. As E. F. Schumacher says, "When we think, we do not just think: we think with ideas. Our mind is not a blank, a *tabula rasa*. When we begin to think we can do so only because our mind is already filled with all sorts of ideas *with which* to think."[3] These "more or less fixed ideas" we *think with* constitute our mental model of the world—in other words, our world view.

What are the major slots in our filing cabinet? Essentially they include these basic concepts: (1) our concept of the most real thing in existence (our notion of *God* or of *ultimate reality*); (2) our view of the essential nature of the external world (ordered or chaotic, material or spiritual); (3) our idea of who we and others really are (our concept of *human nature*); this includes our idea of how we know (*epistemology*) and our notion of what happens to us after we die; (4) our understanding of the good (*ethics*); and (5) our understanding of the meaning of humanity's sojourn on earth (*the meaning of history*).

A world view, in other words, is a map of reality; like any map it may fit what is really there or it may be grossly misleading. The map is not the world itself, of course, only an image of it, more or less accurate in some places, distorted in others. Still all of us carry around such a map in our mental make-up, and we act on it. All of our thinking presupposes it. Most of our experience fits into it. That which does not challenges us to modify our world view, or our world view prevents us from accepting the experience as veridical —really reflecting the way things are.

When writers write they do so from the perspective of their own world view. What they presuppose about themselves, God, the good life and the validity of human knowledge governs both what they say and how they say it. That is why reading with world views in mind (your own and that of the author) will help you understand not only what is written in the lines but what is written between the lines— that is, what is presupposed before a pen ever reaches the page.

Some very good examples of this cry at us from billboards, magazine ads and TV commercials:

You only go 'round once in life. So you've got to grab for all the gusto you can get.

Every TV sports addict knows that one by heart. The advertisement, of course, goes on to say we should drink Schlitz because if you don't drink Schlitz you don't get all the gusto you can. Leaving aside the question of whether Schlitz or any beer really gives *gusto* (relish, zest, keen enjoyment, says one dictionary), look at the argument itself and what must be assumed to be true if the argument is to be accepted.

Item 1: *You only go 'round once in life.* This is a proposition about human nature. Human beings are born, live, die and do not come back. Obviously it rejects any idea of reincarnation.

But notice Item 2: *So you've got to grab for all the gusto you can get.* For this to follow from Item 1, Item 1 must not only reject reincarnation but any kind of life after death. For if there were some kind of life after death, then gusto here might not be appropriate under some circumstances. There might be greater gusto beyond. So Item 1 is really an assumption of naturalism. It will not square at all with the Christian view of human nature. For a Christian there is a life beyond, one where the gusto will be greater than any offered here—even if it is true that Schlitz has gusto.

We might further observe that the Schlitz ad, even for naturalists, singles out one value as primary—enjoyment. It is an appeal to our hedonistic, self-centered nature. A principled naturalist who values others as much as himself should be no more satisfied with this ad than Christians who place the gratification of purely physical desires relatively low on their scale of values.

Lest we think that only a beer commercial could be so crass, could take such a low view of human nature, try the same analysis on the Coca-Cola ad:

Coke adds life. Everybody wants a little life.

Or this ad for a fur coat:

Mink. One of life's great lessons in the fine art of accepting pleasure.

Or this ad for a calculator:

Buy this for someone. Then give it to yourself.

Every argument—and ads are arguments (good or bad, valid or invalid, moral or immoral)—presupposes a common ground with the person to whom it is directed, a ground not in question. This is why pleasure-oriented people will respond to arguments for pleasure-producing things. It is also why arguments directed at one person will not work with someone else. Not enough is shared in common.

Often, however, some presuppositions of a writer may go

undetected because much of wh
patently true we never notice (
wise cause us to raise question
Clark has written that the socia
help us out of our modern predicame.
blow ourselves off the face of the earth. If w
some way of controlling our aggression, mankind
whole may not survive much longer. Clark writes, "Given
the urgency of this immediate survival problem, the psychological and social sciences must enable us to control the
animalistic, barbaric and primitive propensities in man and
subordinate them to the uniquely human moral and ethical
characteristic of love, kindness and empathy."[4]

We see that Clark's values and ours are similar: love,
kindness, empathy. And we have a general respect for
science, especially in the service of humanity. So we may
think to ourselves as we read this, How true, how true! But
have we noticed what Clark has said about what our problem is? We have, he says, a tendency to be *animalistic, barbaric, primitive*. These terms all point to Clark's underlying
assumption—one which governs most thinking in the social
sciences today—that the human race is evolving. The problem is that we have not yet evolved far enough. We must
hasten the evolutionary process by scientifically manipulat-
ing human nature.

Clark's own proposal in his essay (which comes from a
national address to his fellow psychologists) is to manufac-
ture a tranquilizer, a "peace pill," which could be given to
all those with the power to trigger an atomic explosion to
keep them from pushing the button. In a later passage his
assumption of an evolutionary model is made explicit. He
says that the development of such psychotechnology will
give us "the time necessary to evolve and stabilize those
centers of his [man's] brain which will make social morality

man survival no longer a matter of chance."[5] But if
re good readers, we do not need to be told that Clark
umes an evolutionary model for the human race. For he
as tipped his hand much earlier.

We may feel, however, that our problems as human beings do not stem from an incomplete evolution but, say,
from a fallen nature. If, in other words, we assume the
biblical notion that humanity was created perfect in the first
place and that our problem is not the fact that we are animalistic (animals are neither moral nor immoral) or barbaric (not properly cultured; actually just a member of the
wrong culture) or primitive (Adam and Eve were created
perfect), then Clark's proposal is certainly questionable.
The Bible puts the nature of our problem in moral terms:
we rebelled against God. Our trouble is our moral character
not our physical nature or our improper culture.

Detecting the presuppositions of others, therefore, is
vitally important. It is a part of reading well. It puts our own
world view to the test and it gives us a contact with the mind
and heart of those we read and listen to. We begin, then, to
come alive to the vast array of gods and goddesses vying
for our worship, calling for our commitment. And we can
better understand what to think and how to live in a culture
growing ever more decadent.

It isn't just in prose that we need to be aware of world
views. There is a frequent misconception about poetry.
Poetry, we hear people say, is just for emotion and feeling.
Indeed poetry does involve emotion and feeling, but at its
best it reflects our whole character. As Samuel Taylor
Coleridge once said, "No man was ever yet a great poet
without at the same time being a profound philosopher.
For poetry is the blossom and the fragrancy of all human
knowledge, human thoughts, human passions, emotions,
language."[6]

Look, for example, at these two brief lyric poems. The first is by Stephen Crane (1871-1900).

Should the wide world roll away,
Leaving black terror,
Limitless night,
Not God, nor man, nor place to stand
Would be to me essential,
If thou and thy white arms were there,
And the fall to doom a long way.

What view of ultimate value and meaning does Crane express? All the meaning of human life is in the love between a man and a woman. To have that is to be able to withstand the destruction of all else but one's own self. Yet there is much more in these lines than this simple answer to life's profound question of meaning. There is tension and terror, a black backdrop against which one sole, light figure stands starkly revealed. No final resting place but doom is envisioned for the soul. No reason is given for the one value Crane affirms, but we are clear about that affirmation.

Perhaps one reason why world-view issues are present in so much poetry is that poets so often combine two subjects close to the hearts of all of us—love and death. In the following poem by Emily Dickinson (1830-1886) the subject is the same as that in Crane's poem, but there is much more doubt about the answer.

I reason, earth is short,
And anguish, absolute.
And many hurt;
But what of that?

I reason, we could die;
The best vitality
Cannot excel decay;

But what of that?

I reason that in heaven
Somehow, it will be even,
Some new equation given;
But what of that?

Brief, clipped, like three snapshots each recording a state of
mind, this poem captures and compresses the essence of the
poet's thoughts on death—and thus on human significance.
Read the poem again, and then again to capture its poignant reminder of how little we sometimes know.

These two poems, of course, provide only glimpses of a
larger whole from which they come. Crane and Dickinson
have much more to say than this about the meaning of life.
And we as readers have much more to learn about how to
receive their "messages" than I have even hinted. My point
in this section has been simply to illustrate what it means to
read with the mind engaged, what it means to read in the
light of world-view issues.

Where We Are Going
The plan of this book is simple. Chapter two considers how
to read straightforward nonfiction in such a way that we see
not only what the writer intended but also the intellectual
background from which he writes, that is, what he presupposes to be true before he sets forth his case. From this
will come a set of principles for reading any and all kinds of
nonfictional works.

Chapter three discusses how to read poetry with depth of
understanding, and chapter four takes up fiction—short
stories and novels.

Chapter five explains the relevance of the biographical,
literary, historical and intellectual contexts in which written
works participate and which influence their meaning.

Finally, chapter six suggests how you can know when and what to read. The appendix proposes a basic starter plan.

Note: Some of you may wish to read the chapter on poetry or the one on fiction prior to reading the chapter on non-fiction. This can be done without much difficulty. There are references in these chapters to the general discussion of world views in chapter two. You may wish then to refer back to that material when this topic is mentioned.

Some may wonder why I have not made prominent mention of Bible reading. There are two reasons for this. First, there are already many excellent books on how to read or study the Bible.[7] But there is a more important reason: if we learn to read nonfiction, poetry and fiction well, we are automatically equipped to read the Bible very well. To be sure, there are some important aspects unique to reading Scripture and I discuss these on pages 146-48. But reading well is a rather universally applicable craft.

How to Read Slowly
Finally, I want to introduce a motif we will find repeated throughout this book. Reading speed is totally irrelevant. In fact, over and over in the next few chapters I will ask you to read and then re-read. At that rate your speed will be abysmal. If you think you can learn to read well without doing this, I ask you to re-read anyway. I am not insulting your intelligence by doing this. Good readers re-read many things many times.

When you have absorbed the techniques of reading well, you will automatically find your speed increasing. Don't take pride in this. The task we set before ourselves now has nothing to do with quantity. Senator Proxmire, some say, reads two thousand five hundred words a minute. So what? The average reader reads about two hundred fifty words a minute. That is fast enough.

Hamlet: *What a piece of work is man!*
how noble in reason! how infinite
in faculty! in form and moving how
express and admirable! in action how like
an angel! in apprehension how like
a god! And yet to me, what is this
quintessence of dust?
Shakespeare, Hamlet

[Joseph Wood] Krutch has argued that
whereas the traditional view supports
Hamlet's exclamation, "How like a god!,"
Pavlov, the behavioral scientist,
emphasized "How like a dog!" But that
was a step forward. A god is the
archetypal pattern of an explanatory
fiction, of a miracle-working mind,
of the metaphysical. Man is much more
than a dog, but like a dog he is within
the range of scientific analysis.
B. F. Skinner, Beyond Freedom and
Dignity

Chapter 2
Good-By, Professor Ptolemy: Reading Nonfiction

When we pick up a newspaper or a book or an article, we come to our task with certain preconceptions and predispositions. We expect to find a specific piece of information or be presented with an argument or an analysis of something, say, the likelihood of a recession in the next six months or the reasons why Johnny can't read. We probably know a little about the book or article we are reading even before we start. There was, after all, some reason why we chose to read one piece of writing rather than another.

Our expectations and predispositions may, however, blind us to what the article and its author are actually saying. If, for example, we are used to disagreeing with the author, we may see only what we expect to see and not what is actually there. Day after day in our routine pattern of life we expose ourselves to the same newspaper, the same magazines, even books by authors with the same perspectives. In order to reflect on our reading habits and improve our skills we need to break out of this routine, step back and look at what we are doing when we read.

To begin with, then, I want to present an essay that will not be familiar to most readers of this book. It appeared in *The Chronicle of Higher Education,* a weekly newspaper devoted to issues of importance to college and university teachers and administrators. This particular essay, however, is of more general interest. The author, Pamela McCorduck, is assistant professor of English at the University of Pittsburgh.

The topic which McCorduck treats is vital to our self-understanding as human beings in twentieth-century culture. It is one whose implications we must grasp if we are to be aware of who we are and where we are going as individuals and as a society. Moreover, as Christians we will not find ourselves neutral toward McCorduck's remarks or her particular hope for the future.

Nevertheless, as we examine her essay carefully, we are not doing so to comment primarily on the validity of her analysis or the viability of her proposal. Our purpose is at once more basic and in the long run more helpful.

In this chapter we will discuss how to "read" or to "listen," how to see behind what is said, how to read "between the lines" what the "lines" themselves indicate is there. Or, to put it in other terms, we will learn how to read *world-view-ishly.* That is an awkward term, but I don't know how better to express what we should do when we read for comprehension, that is, when we read for any other purpose than pure diversion or entertainment.

Our goal in reading carefully is not only to understand what is being said explicitly but to see as well why it is being said. We want to learn to recognize the world views of writers and speakers, and thus to know what their basic assumptions about life really are. It will help us decide what kind of attention to pay to their specific comments or proposals no matter how modest or immodest.

The Act of Reading: An Example
In reading world-viewishly, we must first pay attention to precisely what is being said. We want to read only what is there and not what we guess ought to be there because we think it is true or because we think it is what such a writer would say.

So, with previous biases consciously set aside, let us read McCorduck's essay.

An Introduction to the Humanities with Prof. Ptolemy
Pamela McCorduck
[1] For its day, the Ptolemaic system was a sophisticated and useful model of the universe. With its cycles and epicycles, it predicted when the known planets would be at a given point in the heavens, and you could navigate quite nicely with it, get yourself from Alexandria to Crete or anywhere else you wanted to go in the Mediterranean. The problem came when people wanted to go beyond Gibraltar. The geocentric model was no longer useful, and the agonized cries of the churchmen did nothing to stop—or aid—the sailors.

[2] The humanities, with their man-centered value system, may now be in the same trouble.

[3] This year my students and I have been reading through some of the more visionary literature of science, and twice we have come across the phrase "human chauvinsim." It is used by biologist Lewis Thomas in his *Lives of a Cell* and by the astronomer Carl Sagan in his *Cosmic Con-*

nection. In quite different ways, both scientists are saying that our exaltation of our own species is as parochial as the white man's burden—another notion that sprang from minds educated in the liberal, humanistic tradition. Not only is it parochial; this exaltation is wantonly destructive of other forms of life around us. And since we treat the life around us with such shortsighted irreverence, we deserve the destruction we are slowly bringing upon ourselves.

[4] Sagan imagines us meeting extraterrestrial intelligences and seems not to know whether to laugh or cry at our probable response. My own interest is in machine intelligence, and I too can make some predictions. When introduced to the idea that a machine can think, the first reaction of many humanists is to laugh. It is preposterous, they say. The very idea that a *thing,* so patently non-human, could claim the most human of properties, the capacity to think, is good for laughs, but nothing more. When they are shown the existence of non-human cognition, in chimpanzees or dolphins, or even in the first primitive computer programs (which certainly do things we would call thinking if humans did them), they mull it over. They know they can re-define thinking as something only humans can do, but that doesn't seem quite fair. Finally they smile and announce with confidence: "Well, we can always pull the plug, can't we?"

[5] The complacency and philistine destructiveness in that answer can be understood only with reference to a man-centered universe. Such a model does not admit that chimpanzees, dolphins, intelligent machines, or extraterrestrial beings might have something valuable to teach us or might even be enormously bored by all our antics.

[6] Not all my colleagues in the humanities feel this way, of course. In my own department there are quite a few of us who see the low pay and the low status afforded the humanities and the graduate students who can't get jobs. We

suspect it's futile to postulate a wicked materialistic system Out There that stubbornly refuses to allow the scales to fall from its eyes and see our true value. Instead, we wonder if what's Out There hasn't indeed measured our value—or values—and found the humanities to be, at the most charitable, obsolete.

[7] A long exchange between C. P. Snow and F. W. R. Leavis—a gentleman's quarrel, really—about the relative merits of science and the humanities is instructive, and it is worth quoting Leavis, speaking for the humanities:

[8] "When human ends require to be pondered in relation to the pressing problems and opportunities with which our civilization faces us, one's thinking should not be blind to the insights given in cultural tradition—on the contrary, it should be informed with the knowledge of basic human need that is transmitted by *that*."

[9] Leavis uses the terms "human ends" and "human need," though even he might agree with most of us that the humanities have rather served the needs of elderly white men as opposed to humanity in general.

[10] More important, Leavis expresses in this passage a fundamental tenet of humanism, one that got it under way as a mode of thinking in the first place. It is that somehow, by rummaging through the follies and triumphs of our ancestors, we will learn something, and go and sin no more. It seems logical that we should learn lessons from history; we keep wishing it were so. I shared that belief for a long time, and I still wish it were the case. But it isn't; it never was; and much blood has been shed as proof of that.

[11] Let us imagine that the movers and shakers on our side of the Vietnam war had each been provided with a copy of Robert Graves's retelling of the Greek myths, and those pages leading up to and including the Trojan War had been dog-eared so nobody should miss the point. Agamemnon's

arrogance about his honor might have been underlined in red, and his willful sacrifice of his own daughter to that end might have earned a handwritten exclamation point in the margin. Would it really have changed the course of the Vietnam war a whit? (And since most of the movers and shakers were products of, and participants in, our most humanities-sodden universities, it's fair to assume that they already knew about the Trojan War without anyone's having to send them books in the mail. Regardless of how pretty the parallels were, *it simply didn't matter.*)

[12] There's no harm in looking at what our species has done in the past; indeed, it's very entertaining and often appalling; but we must stop pretending that we really learn anything from such examinations, or even that we can reform ourselves by such study. We reform ourselves in the present, not the past, adapting ourselves to present needs. Of course we have a sense of history, but what overwhelms us at the moment are the differences, not the similarities. If the past has something to say to us, we seldom pay attention. That may be wicked, wasteful, and wayward, but it is demonstrably the case. Why do we keep kidding ourselves?

[13] In the same essay, Leavis rhapsodizes about "a full intelligent possession of my full humanity . . . something with the livingness of the deepest vital instinct, as intelligence, a power—rooted strong in experience and supremely human—of creative response to the new challenges of time. . . ."

[14] When I read this passage aloud to my students and asked them what it meant, they laughed. I confess I laughed with them. "If we wrote that on our papers . . ." one of my students began, and there was no need for her to continue. I would write *rubbish* in the margin, just as I am writing *rubbish* along many a margin of what I have been brought up—no, trained—to believe is the best that has

been thought and said in the world.

[15] The humanities are demoralized because they are no longer adequate for us in the world as it is. We are hard up for a Copernican revolution, which will take man from the center of the universe and put him someplace more appropriate. There were some valuable things we learned when we were going through our humanist stage, and we surely want to carry those along with us (one of them being that a good replacement for the center of the universe is *not* a parental deity who's going to fix everything up for us in the end). We might want to restate humanist values in such a way as to extend them to all members of our species, and to members of other species besides. But some of our most cherished beliefs are the ones that must go: for a start, we are going to have to jettison the idea of human superiority and come to grips with the idea that complexity is not necessarily superiority, that might is not necessarily right.

[16] To find the humanities wanting is not anti-human. I am as anxious for my species to survive as anyone; I am a human being, I can't be anything else even if I wished it. But you can feel affection and even honor for your species without being carried away by human chauvinism, as I'm afraid so much of the humanities has been.

[17] At the moment I have no idea what might occupy the center of the new universe. Surely it will do us no harm to meditate on that vacancy, and perhaps try out various candidates. For all I know, some neo-Copernicus is sitting on a startling new model right now, refining it quietly and methodically, unwilling to publish until the safety of the deathbed is at hand. Maybe the new model will be delivered to us by some extraordinary invention of our own, an offspring in the form of a computer program whose imagination, if I may use that word, has long outpaced that of its creators, as offspring will. Or maybe that new model is here,

under our noses, waiting for us to install it in place of man-the-measure-of-all-things.[1]□

On first reading, McCorduck's essay may be baffling. But don't despair. How many books or articles have you read lately that talk about education—its purposes or function in society? Only English teachers, scientists and students of the humanities are likely to have heard of C. P. Snow, F. W. R. Leavis or Robert Graves. No matter. The writing is clear enough and the essay is short—even if a bit complicated. So why not re-read it, now, before going on? After all, this is a book about how to read slowly!

On a second reading we may still feel that the essay is not as clear to us as we would like it to be. Nevertheless, it is our job to understand what McCorduck has said, and if that means untangling her argument or puzzling out her references to a couple of ancient astronomers, then so be it.

If this book were primarily about "good" writing and "bad" writing, we would want to pause, at least occasionally, for judgment. We would ask as we analyzed the writing, "Has McCorduck done her job well as a writer? Is she always clear and lucid? Has she presumed too much prior knowledge on our part? Are her thoughts well organized and presented in the dress of appropriate diction and sentence structure? Has she presented her case clearly and powerfully?" But as readers we rarely have the luxury of such value judgments. Often we are forced by circumstances to read a book or an article, regardless of how poorly written, when we have no desire to do so. True, for our own unforced reading we will tend (and should tend) to select books which are both helpful for what they say and a joy for how they say it. In school, however, or on the job, we find ourselves struggling with writing that demands close attention if not hard work. How do we live with that?

Clarifying the Vocabulary

One of the first steps in defogging the prose—if we find it foggy—is to clarify the vocabulary. Social scientists, for example, often use technical terminology. English teachers, perhaps in an attempt to emulate their master, William Shakespeare whose vocabulary is the largest on record (some twenty-two thousand words), are also prone to use a sophisticated vocabulary.

Obviously if we do not understand the words McCorduck uses, we will not understand her. Our first step as readers, therefore, is to consult a good dictionary to discern the meaning of the terms we do not know. So we can keep together on our analysis here, let me list some brief definitions of a few of her more arcane terms. Actually, in the case of McCorduck's essay the diction is for the most part quite ordinary. If you already know some of the terms I define, please bear with me or skip to the next section. The following terms are given in the order of appearance in the essay; the number in brackets refers to the paragraph in which the term is first used.

epicycle [1]: "In the Ptolemaic system, a small circle whose center moves on the circumference of a larger circle having the earth as its center (the deferent), while its own circumference describes the orbit of a planet" (*Funk and Wagnalls Standard College Dictionary,* hereafter referred to as SCD; in this particular dictionary there is a small diagram which makes this description quite clear; try your own dictionary. What do you find?)

humanities [2]: the area of studies that includes literature, history, philosophy, the fine arts; to be distinguished from the sciences.

chauvinism [3]: unreasoning attachment to one's own nation, race or group; deriving from Nicholas Chauvin, an overzealous supporter of Napoleon.

parochial [3]: narrow, restricted in scope.

white man's burden [3]: "The alleged duty of the white peoples to spread culture among the so-called backward peoples of the world: phrase originated by Rudyard Kipling" (SCD).

extraterrestrial intelligences [4]: beings from beyond the earth who possess intelligence.

cognition [4]: thought, thinking.

philistine [5]: "An ignorant, narrow-minded person, devoid of culture and indifferent to art" (SCD).

Closely related to possible problems in vocabulary are difficulties of assumed knowledge. No writer begins by thinking of his or her readers as totally empty vessels. All take it for granted that their readers bring with them a wealth of knowledge—not only an implicit knowledge of the language but also a store of facts and opinions, information and attitudes. Just how much writers assume their readers already know determines the *level* of their writing. Professional psychologists writing for their colleagues may be able to say, as Kenneth B. Clark has, that "moral verbalizations of the past have been prostituted by the pathos of power; they have been perverted by the pretenses of rationality in service of inhumanity if not barbarity."[2] The rest of us—that is, we nonpsychologists—are going to wonder what a *moral verbalization* is, not to mention the *pathos of power* and the *pretenses of rationality.* Kenneth B. Clark in making that statement did not pause to define his terms for his readers; he assumed they could understand what he was saying.

Catching the Allusions

Pamela McCorduck, too, assumes we know a great deal. This is nowhere more evident than her assumption that we have a passing knowledge of Ptolemy and his geocentric system of astronomy; that we know it was challenged by

Copernicus whose revolutionary system placed the sun rather than the earth at the center of the universe. If we don't know or remember this, again a dictionary will help to remind us. True, we can learn that Ptolemy was a second-century Greek astronomer living in Alexandria, and that his "ancient astronomical system . . . assumed that the earth was the central body around which the sun, planets and celestial bodies revolved" (SCD). Likewise, we can learn about Copernicus and his system. Moreover, if we do not know where Alexandria is, or Crete or Gibraltar or even the Mediterranean, the necessary basic information is only a dictionary away.

I have dwelled on this topic rather longer than I would have liked. It seems so obvious to me—and thus to be an insult to you, my own readers. But I know how important it is to catch the precision of a writer's thought and how easy it is to get help from a dictionary. And I know how long it took me as a reader before I made a habit of consulting one. I was in graduate school. Enough said?

Still, a dictionary will not solve all our problems. It just makes their solution by other means possible. For example, the references to Ptolemy and Copernicus are not just allusions to facts or people or events from the past. Mc-Corduck introduces her whole argument by reference to a major revolution in human thought that occurred a few centuries ago. It is important for us as readers to realize that the Copernican revolution involved a radical reordering of the way we as human beings saw ourselves in relation to God and the universe. To fully appreciate the flavor and force of her own proposal we need to be more than casually aware of the history of ideas.

In one sense, a person has to know everything in order to know anything. And that, of course, is impossible. So as readers we do the best we can. If McCorduck is the first to introduce us to the idea that there was a major shift in human thought at the time of Copernicus (the sixteenth century), then let us remember this when we read similar essays. Or let us go to our library and begin to dig into Ptolemy and Copernicus to find out if McCorduck is right to use them and their theories as a base for her own argument. Or let us do as usually we must (for we can't track down everything)—realize we do not have all the information we would like to have but strive to use what we do have to best advantage. As we continue to read carefully, we will find ourselves more and more able to read material written for a more and more knowledgeable audience.

When we have clarified McCorduck's terminology, we are ready to tackle her argument. To do this we will ask ourselves a series of questions. As the answers to each of these unfold, we will discover that our answers to the other questions are becoming more rich and subtle, in short, both more detailed and more accurate. Gradually we will come to see the system of ideas that underlies the whole essay. In other words, we will come to see what her world view is.

Four Primary Questions
Here are the first four primary questions. We will consider each in turn:
  1. What *genre* (kind of writing) is McCorduck's essay?
  2. What is the *thesis* (main idea) of the essay?
  3. What *evidence* or arguments does McCorduck give for her thesis, and how is this evidence organized?
  4. What *objections* to her thesis does McCorduck consider, and how does she respond to these possible objections?
After we have answered these questions, we will have a better idea which further ones to ask. Obviously an essay on violence on TV will not consider the same issues as an es-

say on the folk cures for plantar warts, and so the questions we ask in reading world-viewishly will be different for each piece of writing. Let us turn, then, to the first four questions.

1. The *genre* of McCorduck's writing is argument; that is, McCorduck is explaining a situation (in this case a human predicament, the loss of a central reference point to our human self-understanding), and she is calling (perhaps *longing* would be a better word) for someone, somewhere, to present us with a new central reference point.

It is important to observe that McCorduck is serious; she is not writing comedy, poking fun, cajoling, haranguing, exhorting, reminiscing, posing a witty conundrum or exposing a human foible.

The tone of comic writing, for example, is very different from that in McCorduck's essay. Consider this paragraph from an article entitled, "The UFO Menace":

All UFOs may not prove to be of extraterrestrial origin, but experts do argue that any glowing cigar-shaped aircraft capable of rising straight up at twelve miles per second would require the kind of maintenance and sparkplugs available only on Pluto. If these objects are indeed from another planet, then the civilization that designed them must be millions of years more advanced than our own. Either that or they are very lucky. Professor Leon Speciman postulates a civilization in outer space that is more advanced than ours by approximately fifteen minutes. This, he feels, gives them a great advantage over us, since they needn't rush to get to appointments.[3]

No one can mistake the comedic touch here. Woody Allen may be exposing what he sees to be a human foible—our gullibility for the sensational, but he certainly has kept us from taking him straight: a dash of bitters, a twist of lemon, on the rocks, maybe, but not straight.

McCorduck, on the other hand, tells us by her tone that in this essay we are to be a serious people bent on a serious business. All the rest of the questions we ask and the answers we give assume that McCorduck is presenting a straightforward case for her thesis.

2. We have already mentioned the *thesis* (main idea) of McCorduck's essay in our answer to question 1: The Western world has lost its confidence in the traditional, humanist (man-centered) basis of value and has nothing to put in its place. This is a serious loss and calls for an open-minded attempt to discover a new center of value.

Put so baldly and abstractly, McCorduck's central "message" is cold, lifeless. We may wonder why all the fuss. What is so important about a central, unifying value? Actually, McCorduck has identified the most important issue we face as human beings. In secular terms she is raising the same point as Joshua some three thousand years ago as he addressed the Israelites just before he died. "Choose this day whom you will serve," he said, "whether the gods your fathers served . . . or the gods of the Amorites" (Josh. 24: 15). Nothing is more important than knowing where ultimate reality lies—the really real and the really good, that is, the infinite reality beyond all finite reality and the absolute good beyond all local values. What modern "god" shall we serve?

But when I allude to Joshua, for Christians I pump emotional tone into plain philosophy, life into abstract thought. And this is precisely what McCorduck does with her opening references to Ptolemy and the Copernican revolution. How, then, has she structured her thought and given it vitality?

3. The *evidence* McCorduck uses to substantiate her thesis is not, of course, detailed or well developed. But it

covers a broad spectrum, and it is just this breadth that will allow us eventually to see what her world view is. Let us summarize the flow of her argument from beginning to end.

McCorduck begins by reminding her readers of what she assumes they already know—that the Ptolemaic system worked in a limited area but not beyond it. It couldn't solve some problems people insisted on solving and so was jettisoned as soon as a better system came along. All this is presented, we then learn in paragraph 2, as an analogy: "the humanities, with their man-centered value system, may now be in the same trouble." Then comes the evidence:

(1) People like Lewis Thomas and Carl Sagan are now decrying "human chauvinism"; intelligent species other than mankind may inhabit the universe and they have an equal claim to value [paragraph 3].

(2) Chimpanzees, dolphins and computers are now seen to be capable of thought; they have an equal claim to value [paragraphs 4-5].

(3) Ironically, some humanities teachers admit they have been weighed and found wanting [paragraph 6].

(4) The quarrel between C. P. Snow and F. W. R. Leavis shows us that the humanities, naively believing that we learn from literature or history, have no power to affect anyone for the good—even students of the humanities [paragraphs 7-12]. McCorduck details this argument by noting that those in charge of the Vietnam war were graduates (she says "products") of universities where the humanities are highly respected. Knowledge of "Agamemnon's arrogance about honor" was of no help. History is of interest to us, but it teaches us nothing; we are creatures of the moment, "adapting ourselves to present needs" [paragraph 12].

(5) The moral pronouncements of modern humanist

pundits (Leavis is again the example) are upon reflection—even by her own students—only rubbish. What the humanities claim to be the best that has been thought and said in the world is no better [paragraphs 13-15].

(6) We need a new center of value—not man and not God (whom she characterizes as "a parental deity who's going to fix everything up for us in the end"). Perhaps it could be a dechauvinized humanism, perhaps something quite outside our present purview [paragraphs 15-16].

(7) We should meditate on the "vacancy" and try new centers. These could come from several places—a contemporary genius, or a computer whose imagination has exceeded that of its "creators." Perhaps the new center is already here waiting for someone to notice it [paragraph 17].

To outline and summarize every essay and book we read is, of course, impossible and usually unnecessary. Keeping track of the flow of the argument with notes in the margin or on a pad of paper will generally suffice. But when you know you need to read especially carefully, writing out the skeleton argument as above will certainly crystallize the material in your own mind and make answering the tougher world-view questions much easier.

4. McCorduck is aware that we may have some *objections* to her argument. Two are considered. In paragraphs 4 and 5 she notes that some people do not believe machines should be accorded human value (at least at the point of thinking). They say, "Well, we can always pull the plug, can't we?" Her response is to note the "philistine destructiveness" in the answer and to counter with the charge that it makes sense to do that only in a man-centered universe. In other words her response involves name calling and a simple restatement of her thesis.

In some ways we could consider the bulk of paragraphs 7-14 as a response to Leavis. It is cast as a rejoinder to a prior argument by him. Other than this, she carries on little dialog with those who might disagree with her. She quickly presents her case and leaves it at that.

As we survey the essay we see more clearly that Mc-Corduck has made broad, sweeping claims, thrown down a challenge to her colleagues in English, history and philosophy, and then quickly left the field. Obviously there is more to say on this topic, and we know from what she intimates here that she is well aware of that. But limited by space—no essay in this section of *The Chronicle of Higher Education* can be much longer—she has played out her argument and we as readers are left to learn from it, evaluate it and, if only in our own minds, thoughtfully respond.

But first we need to dig deeper. We need to read between the lines and try to see why she feels this argument is valid, its conclusion true, its hope realistic.

Identifying the Author's World View
Every argument presupposes a base, explicit or implicit, something assumed that is not at the moment in question. Our ground-floor assumptions—ones that are so basic that none more basic can be conceived—compose our world view. As I have already indicated in chapter one, there are only a limited number of basic areas that require ground-floor assumptions. Among them are *being* (what is ultimately real), *knowing* (how we know), *morality* (what is the ultimate good), *human nature* (who or what we are) and *human significance* (the value of humanity and the meaning of history). So, when we look for an author's world view we look for the assumptions he or she makes in these areas. If we find these assumptions faulty or questionable, we know that the argument itself must be rejected or at least held in doubt until we have resolved our questions.

What happens, then, when we ask of McCorduck's

essay the following basic world-view questions?

5. What does McCorduck consider to be prime reality—the really real?

6. What is the nature of humanity?

7. What is the basis for morality?

8. What is the meaning of human history?

Again, let us consider each in turn.

5. The question of prime reality is at the heart of McCorduck's essay. It is, as I mentioned above, the basic issue treated. What, after all, is the beginning of all our thought and final resting place for all our questions?

The negative answers McCorduck discusses are identified clearly. The humanists, she says, put man as the prime reality—man, the measure of all things.

God, that "parental deity," is mentioned but dismissed in a parenthesis. If he ever was at the center, he has not been there for some time. Surely, McCorduck must know that culturally speaking indeed God was at the center. From the first few centuries A.D. to the Renaissance in the fifteenth through the seventeenth centuries (broadly considered), the Christian God was considered the kingpin of all reality; he was seen as the great I AM, the self-existent One from whom and by whom and through whom all else exists. But much can be read from the tone as well as the content of McCorduck's one allusion to God. She reduces God to a convenient fixer up of cosmic wrongs. It is fair to say she does not begin to wrestle with the God of the Bible as the medieval and Reformation theologians did and as serious Christians still do today. The God of Abraham, Isaac and Jacob is not the petty, household God McCorduck seems to imagine. Still, it is obvious that McCorduck feels it would be a waste of time to reconsider the traditional Judeo-Christian notion of God. She only mentions him in a slighting way, I would surmise, so that no one will think she is a reactionary and wants to go back to a centering notion we have done well to abandon. McCorduck may be a disillusioned humanist, but she is certainly no closet Christian.

But man, too, McCorduck dismisses. Her focus here is on man as valuer and value maker. In other words, her main argument concerns ethics not metaphysics. And well she should limit humanism to ethics, for secular humanism has never had an explanation for how man could *be* the prime reality itself. He is finite—both individually and collectively. Once mankind did not exist. Now mankind exists. Someday mankind will again not be. Without a personal origin as a being made by God, man is left only with an impersonal origin. He is a piece of the natural universe that somehow— no one knows how or can ever know how—became conscious of itself and developed self-determination. But he is unlike anything else he has yet observed. So far he does not see personality reflected other than dimly in his machines— whether they compute (and thus think) or not.

This as human beings we do know: we are not a transcendent God who brought all this cosmos to pass. We are not prime reality. We are born, live and die; we are finite. Prime reality must be infinite; it must be that which is, always has and always will be.

So what then shall we say about McCorduck's prime reality? She claims to know what it is not—man or a personal God, but she admits that she does not know for sure what it might be. Still, she gives some interesting hints. Humanity might share the role with others—other species like dolphins, chimpanzees and extraterrestrials, and other things like thinking machines [paragraphs 5, 15]. Are these, individually or collectively, infinite?

The problem is one of alternatives. There aren't many. Either prime reality is transcendent (that is, a god beyond) or it is immanent (equal with the cosmos). McCorduck has ruled out the first. Therefore prime reality is immanent.

Then there are only two further possibilities: either this prime reality is personal (having self-reflection and self-determination) or impersonal (just there as an ordered realm). Here McCorduck is ambiguous. Humanity is not equal to the cosmos; that rules out that evidence for a personal prime reality. But the possibility for personality is still there. Is this why she has hope? Could it be that from the wellsprings of some cosmic personality a new centering force will come to help us integrate our lives and give us a way to measure our merit as men and women? If not from some personal source, then why the hope? Is McCorduck waiting for the impersonal to break through with a personal answer? Or is the hope still very much a humanistic one—but just not so chauvinistic? If so, then she must explain—as all naturalistic humanists must—how the finite can ever grasp the infinite with enough surety to fashion a center which is truly the center. That job demands a god—not, just any god but an infinite-personal God, one who knows the whole and who has the interest to share that knowledge with a part of the whole—human beings, us.

This section may seem to have taken us far from McCorduck's essay. But that is not so. McCorduck raises the question of the base of all reality. We have just looked to see what she implies by what she says in answer to her own inquiry. We have been reading world-viewishly, but we have been *reading* not inventing or imagining what is not really there.

6. McCorduck's view of human nature itself is also present, at least in embryo. Human beings are not really as unique as they have thought for the last few centuries. Chimpanzees, dolphins and computers think. (McCorduck offers no evidence of this; from my own reading I would say that some of the evidence is fascinating but that it points

only to rather limited kinds of thought.) Extraterrestrials, whom she assumes may exist, may equal if not surpass man in value. (Again she offers no evidence for the existence of extraterrestrials, though Carl Sagan to whom she refers does argue for their statistical probability in *The Cosmic Connection.*)

Moreover, human beings do not learn from history. We continue to act irresponsibly, though at least some of us know better. That is, even knowledge is not our salvation. "We have a sense of history," she says but we are creatures of the present and adapt ourselves to the local situation. Even our best thinkers speak rubbish.

In McCorduck's view we are caught, it would seem, between a varied group of visions of what we ideally might be and what we actually are. Leavis's goals are romantic, unrealizable, perhaps not even intelligible. McCorduck, on the other hand, is so pessimistic about mankind that her own hope for the future seems out of place. We can understand why she longs for us to do better by ourselves, but in light of her denigration of our abilities on the one hand and the equality we share with some animals and some machines on the other hand, why the hope? In fact, why does she herself have any confidence in her own thinking process? Why should McCorduck believe McCorduck?

Yet she does. And she looks beyond herself to some neo-Copernicus who is perhaps "sitting on a startling new model [of the universe] right now" [paragraph 17]. But McCorduck offers no basis for this hope. As we saw above, the alternatives for such a base are very few. A Christian can see humanity as created by an infinite-personal God in his own image. Thus as Christians we can see why we are valuable. And we can see all humanity now—ourselves included—as in rebellion against God and thus fallen; this explains our fraility, our weakness, our inability to match even our partial knowledge of what is good with our actions. We know something of the good, but we fail to live up to our own vision.

McCorduck just has the fact of mankind—first, the paltry record of our straining to know good without a standard by which to measure whether our visions of good are right and, second, the even more tragic record of our failure in the face of any ideals we have ever imagined.

7. The basis for *morality* has already been discussed under the question of the really real. Usually these two issues—the nature of being, the nature of the good—are separate. But McCorduck interweaves the two from the very start by posing the question of a center for human value. As we saw, this took us directly to the issue of prime reality. No further discussion of that is necessary. We need only note that McCorduck admits she does not know what the basis of morality is. It is not man; it is not God. So what is it? Won't someone tell us?

She quotes Leavis as one who would tell us if we would listen. But what she quotes is indeed precisely what she says, a rhapsody of rubbish. Leavis's phrases, "full intelligent possession of my full humanity," "the livingness of the deepest vital instinct," "creative response to the new challenges of time" have no clear meaning at all. And, even if they did, it would be more than fair to ask, whether in light of human history this humanistic vision isn't just a dream. Surely McCorduck is right to reject Leavis for his utterly irrational romanticism. But is she herself not romantic to think that there is someone else or something else in the universe who will tell us?

8. Concerning the meaning of human history, it would likewise seem that McCorduck is agnostic. When a center of value is found, that would provide the basis for an answer. But without that, there is no answer.

In contrast Christians view the meaning of human history as directly related to God's plan and purpose for us.
As he made us, gave us responsibility for our actions and
set up a system of consequences (what Francis Schaeffer
calls a uniformity of cause and effect in an open system),[4]
so history becomes the stage on which God's own drama is
played out. He is the maker of both the stage and the
players. It is his work of art that we are enacting. All seem-
ing lack of meaning and significance is just that—only
apparent. Behind each event stands God's meaning whether we perceive it or not. Contrary to McCorduck, God is not
just a "parental deity" who in the end patches up a job he
botched at the beginning. His majesty permeates the whole
flow of human history. Isaiah in chapters 41—48 gives a
glimpse of God's ways in specific human events, but the
whole Bible from Genesis to Revelation carries the meaning
of the ongoing story of humanity as God wants us to know
it. A Christian can know much about it if he will apply himself to the Bible.

Looking back over our answers to these four world-view
questions, we can, I think, conclude that McCorduck's
world view is naturalism. She has eliminated the possibility
of the existence of God conceived in most traditional senses.
That means she is not a theist or a pantheist. She looks to
the world itself—or some part of the cosmos—to supply our
center of value. Her suggestion that we may be bailed out of
our cultural impasse by an "imaginative" computer program tells us she is not a traditional "humanist." She is,
rather, an optimistic "human" who against high odds is
stretching toward a new ethical base.

In an age when the "new consciousness" world view is
becoming an option, we might expect McCorduck to lean
toward altered states of consciousness for a hint of a new
center of value. She certainly leaves open the door for this,

especially as it is expressed in the countercultural interest in gurus—shamans who know beyond ordinary knowing. I refer here to her allusion to "some neo-Copernicus" [paragraph 17]. But she does not develop this hint, and I may be remiss to so interpret her remark.

There is, then, an open-endedness to McCorduck's world view. More than tainted with a skepticism of all past systems, she finds nowhere to rest—at least at the moment. We are as a culture in a holding pattern or on a quest; we have as men and women—the human race—not arrived. Perhaps with the sloughing off of so many cultural missteps we can now begin.

Reading with a Christian Mind

You will have noticed that as I have raised the last four questions I have found it natural not only to observe Mc-Corduck's answers but to comment from the standpoint of a Christian world view. I have done this to provide a model. I believe it is the duty of all good readers to see what they are reading in the light of their own presuppositions. This does two things.

First it tests on the anvil of experience one's own world view. It is always possible that a person with a different perspective will see what is actually there but we have missed. We certainly should alter our own views when we find they do not fit the way things are. A recognition of our own proneness to error should be a part of every Christian's world view. Our own personal world view as Christians will always have many rough spots and gaps and downright mistakes.

We will consider later how best to build for ourselves a Christian world view (see pp. 146-48). To be sure we do not learn the rudiments of it from naturalists and pantheists. We learn it from the Scripture. But from naturalists and pantheists we may learn things we might otherwise miss. And whatever is true is a part of God's truth; there must be a place for it in our world view.

Second, recognizing the Christian alternative to problems raised in another world view gives us a contact point with those who are not Christians. True, in our discussions with our friends we ought not constantly barrage them with our "better" grasp of the meaning of life. But we should reach out to them where they are, and what better way than to be able to show how Christianity—Christ himself— touches life as it is really lived by all of us, Christian or not?

Looking back over questions 5-8, we might wish to make other observations from a Christian standpoint. But these are enough to illustrate that when we read world-viewishly as Christians, we should be aware that our own world view may suggest alternatives or support specific elements we have discovered as we read carefully. One important value of reading is first to see others as they see themselves and then to see them from a biblical perspective. We thus come to understand better our neighbors, our society, ourselves and even God.

General Principles of Reading World-viewishly

Through our analysis of McCorduck's essay we have seen a practical illustration of reading world-viewishly. It is always possible that techniques and principles employed in one case will not fit others. McCorduck's essay, for example, takes up an issue that raised a number of world-view type questions. Not every essay does that. Is it possible, for instance to read the daily newspaper at this level? Can we discover the world view of a Bernstein or a Woodward from reading their reports in the *Washington Post?* Perhaps yes; perhaps no.

Every essay, every report contains a different set of details, some revealing a specific world view, some not. Of course, every statement written or spoken will reveal something not explicitly stated—for example, the fact of language, the fact of communication and so forth. Each of these eventually fits into the author's ultimate intellectual frame of reference. But not all essayists bare their world view as readily as McCorduck has in this one short piece.

But so be it. Our attempt to read world-viewishly will be amply rewarded as we read the major essays in magazines such as *The Atlantic, Harper's, Saturday Review, Commentary, Esquire, Rolling Stone*—and numerous others. The general essays in *Time* often betray a basic world view, as do editorials in the daily paper and Sunday supplements. In fact, we can learn a great deal about the cultural terrain of our time by reading such material regularly.

Nonfiction books can also be profitably read world-viewishly. And if these books represent important cultural trends or if they are read widely and influence the society around us, reading them world-viewishly can lead us to a profound understanding of our age. Alvin Toffler's *Future Shock,* long on the best-seller charts, informed hundreds of thousands of readers—and it did so from an explicit world view, naturalism. Carlos Castaneda's best sellers, the most recent of which is *The Second Ring of Power,* displays updated animism and new consciousness orientation. So do Theodore Roszak's books such as *Where the Wasteland Ends.* The popular sex manuals often reveal their roots in either naturalism (and more specifically in hedonism) or in some form of Eastern pantheism where the body is sexually tuned to the rhythms of nature and thus becomes an instrument of spiritual as well as physical ecstasy.

World views are evident in fiction and poetry too. Robert Pirsig's *Zen and the Art of Motorcycle Maintenance,* for example, is all about changing one's world view and has almost nothing to do with Zen. Chaim Potok's remarkably readable novels, such as *The Chosen* or *My Name Is Asher Lev,* are fascinating studies in the clash between world views as seen, respectively, by a brilliant, young Jewish scholar and a sensitive young Jewish painter. But this is to encroach on the following chapters.

While each genre of writing requires somewhat different reading techniques, there are, I believe, some helpful principles that apply to most reading. If, as you try to apply these principles to a particular piece, any one of them fails to yield results, abandon it and use what applies.

1. Do not try to read fast; read at your normal rate—or more slowly. Speed reading may be of value for some things, but not for reading world-viewishly.

2. Read with a pen or pencil in hand: underline passages and terms and allusions which the author seems to be most interested in. This will come in handy as you attempt to find the thesis statement and the structure of the argument.

3. If you are reading a book rather than an article or essay, read the preface and any other introductory material. This will often tell you what the author thinks he is doing and may give you valuable insight into his presuppositions, the methods he employs and so forth.

4. Use the dictionary or other reference works such as a desk encyclopedia for *all* words and concepts you do not understand. One way to increase your vocabulary is to write the definition that applies above the word itself. (Here is a side benefit: You will learn to write small!)

5. Underline major organizational words such as *first, second,* etc. This will help you understand the structure of the argument. You may wish to write numbers in the margins alongside important turns in the argument so that later you can grasp the organizational flow. Writing styles differ

so much that each essay will suggest its own method of marginal notation.

6. After reading the essay or chapter, immediately review it and locate the thesis. Most essays or chapters contain one sentence or paragraph or brief section which says in a nutshell what is going to be discussed or has been discussed. Usually this will be either near the beginning or near the end. (In McCorduck's essay the thesis is most fully expressed in the second and the last paragraphs.) Often accompanying the thesis will be a brief, capsule summary of the whole piece. This will provide the focus for your understanding of the whole essay. So underline this section(s) and write *thesis* in the margin.

7. Construct and note in the margin a crude outline of the entire essay or chapter. This is to help you see the *way* the author argues. It may lead you to discern how he thinks and why he believes his reasons are valid. This, as we saw in McCorduck's essay, may lead us to uncover important elements of his world view. With a book it is often helpful to study the table of contents. Some give an elaborate breakdown of the flow of the argument. Even the barest of chapter titles will be of some help to you as you try to discern the general pattern of the book.

8. Determine the genre of the piece you are reading. Ordinarily this is easy and will not sound very important. You know you are reading an essay, a poem, a novel, a drama and so forth. Nonetheless, if a poem is written in the first person, you may want to ask if it is autobiographical or if the poet is writing in persona. Literary forms which cross the boundaries of fiction and history, such as historical novels (*Tale of Two Cities, The Three Musketeers*) and fictionalized history (*The Confessions of Nat Turner, Roots*) also force you to ask questions about what is fact and what is imagination.

You also need to be sure that you have correctly identified the writer's relation to his material. Is he being facetious, satiric, humorous or straight? The stance of the author may vary throughout the piece, and it is important to notice any shifts in approach. Otherwise you may take a satire for serious comment—or vice versa. It is also helpful to ask whether the writer is primarily seeking to inform or to persuade. It will be easier to detect the world view underlying an argument than that underlying a piece which only seeks to inform.

9. Consider if and how the author has achieved his purpose. What kind of evidence docs he draw on? What authorities does he cite? Which does he criticize? Why? What objections does he take into consideration? Does he refute them? How?

Up to this point there has been nothing particularly world-viewish about these reading techniques. They just make good sense, and many people are quite familiar with them. The suggestions which follow, however, are specifically designed to elicit from the text the world view actually embodied there.

A reader cannot answer these questions, however, without first being clear about the essay itself on its own terms. If you jump past the earlier study, you are almost certain to misread when you consider the following crucial issues. While the first eight items are cast as principles or techniques to follow or do, the next items are cast in the form of questions to ask as you closely examine the work you are reading.

10. What does the author consider to be prime reality, the really real? Does he or she believe God exists? What is God like? Is God personal or impersonal, infinite or finite, one or many? What relationship does God have to the cosmos, to human events, to people, to the author himself?

11. What does the author consider to be the nature of the external universe? Is it matter only or spirit only or a combination? Is it basically orderly or chaotic? What causes events or changes in the world?

12. According to the author, what is the nature of humanity? Are human beings personal or impersonal at their most essential? Is a person a machine, an organism, a Gestalt, a spirit or some combination? What, if anything, distinguishes human beings from animals (or other animals)? How are human beings related to God (if he is held to exist)? Do people have control over themselves or are all their actions determined or programmed? If they have free will, how is this possible in light of the nature of God and the universe? What is mankind's essential situation or predicament today? What, if anything, is wrong with a person as an individual or with mankind in society? Is there any solution to mankind's predicament? What? Why will this solution be effective? What is the basis for human knowledge? How is it that we can know and know that we know?

13. According to the author, what happens to a human being at death? Is a person as such annihilated or transformed (into what)? When does a person come into being? Is death the end of all earthly existence? Or is reincarnation a possibility? Under what circumstances?

14. According to the author, what is the basis for morality? This is a more fundamental question than, What values does the author affirm? It gets to the root of all his or her values. Is value only the creation of each person? Of society at large? Of a transcendent God? Is there an absolute good? Where is it found? When values come in conflict, how can the conflict be resolved?

15. According to the author, what is the meaning of history? Does history have any meaning at all? Is history the plan of God? Is the meaning of history the meaning any one

person gives it? Or is it the sum of the meanings all people give it? Is history linear or cyclical; that is, do human events have a uniqueness such that they will never be repeated or do they eternally recur? Is time a meaningful category or do real events happen only in a timeless realm?

If this is the first time you have seen so many tough questions all in one place, you may want to throw up your reading glasses in despair! How can one answer them all? Are you sure that they can be answered by reference to the text? Well, obviously some can be answered and, as we saw with McCorduck's essay, some cannot.

But even if those questions could be answered, would it not take a long time to do so? Yes, at first. Principle 1 is to forget about speed reading. Nonetheless, as you practice reading world-viewishly, you will find it easier and easier. It will probably become second nature. Eventually, you may even be able to speed read world-viewishly—though do not place much credence in what you glean this way. Do not make any decision based on speed reading—any decision at all—except maybe to decide what to read with care. Speed reading is of value only for picking up facts and for eliminating careful reading of some things. For serious business—and even for entertainment—don't play games. Read with your mind.

Theseus:
The lunatic, the lover and the poet
Are of imagination all compact:
One sees more devils than vast hell can hold;
That is the madman: the lover, all as frantic,
Sees Helen's beauty in a brow of Egypt:
The poet's eye in a fine frenzy rolling,
Doth glance from heaven to earth, from earth to
  heaven;
And as imagination bodies forth
The forms of things unknown, the poet's pen
Turns them to shapes and gives to airy nothing
A local habitation and a name.
Shakespeare, A Midsummer Night's Dream

Chapter 3
That Time of Year:
Reading Poetry

Reading poetry requires a different mix of skills and attitudes than reading nonfiction. Both demand from the
reader an open mind and steady attention. But an open
mind and steady attention will find different things in
poetry than in prose. Language is, of course, the medium
for both prose and poetry, but poetry is likely to have a different effect on a reader because it has a different nature
and ordinarily a different goal.

Two Ways to Use Language
First, nonfiction generally employs language in a *philosophic*
way. That is, nonfiction attempts to state directly the nature
of the case or to explain directly why it cannot be so explained. In doing this, a statement in nonfiction at its best

means one thing and one thing only. Each proposition is unilinear; there is no equivocation (all terms always mean the same thing no matter where they occur within the argument) and there is no ambiguity (every term is clearly defined).

In a single work of nonfiction prose any given statement or set of statements is a part of a larger structure of ideas. Each forms one part consistent with however much of the larger whole that has been worked out by the writer. In a well-wrought essay or book there will be no inconsistency between statements in one section and those in another. As a book or essay progresses, there will be development, elaboration, qualification, illustration, application and so forth. But what is said at the end will conform to what was said at the beginning. Whether or not there is unity of form, there will be unity of content.

Poetry, on the other hand, employs language in an *imaginative* or *literary* way. Each word, each image, each sentence, each line and stanza is first a part of a total linguistic structure, and often it will not be well understood until the whole literary structure is present in the mind to act on and qualify the meaning of the part. In poetry, especially, a reader is asked to work harder. He often has to keep more in his mind than a reader of prose nonfiction.

Second, and this must be grasped before poetry can be appreciated, each word, each image, each line and each sentence may well be intentionally ambiguous. It is often supposed to mean more than one thing. Poetic statements are multilinear. When a poor reader of poetry feels a good reader of poetry is "reading between the lines" and thus "creating" his own meaning, he may simply be failing to see what is "in the lines" themselves, having been put there deliberately by the poet. This idea cries out for illustration, and in the pages that follow I hope to document this well.

Finally—and this too is vital—a sentence in poetry states the nature of the case within the terms of the total linguistic structure. Any given "proposition" (and it may be misleading to use such a term with regard to poetic language) may be a description of a fantastical, purely imaginary scene, the dialog of a fictional (even fabulous) character, the explanation of a nonsensical idea and so forth. Furthermore, these sentences may be intended flatly, ironically, whimsically or symbolically. The context will help the reader determine the tone. It may even be that a sentence will have one meaning read flatly and another meaning read ironically, and both may be intended by the author. Both seemingly contradictory meanings may be united in a higher synthesis obvious only when the reader has grasped something of the shape of the total poem.

There is a third important difference between nonfiction prose and imaginative literature. Nonfiction appeals primarily to the mind; the major goal is to *convince* the reader that some state of affairs is or was so, that some idea is or was true, or that some action should or should not be taken. Nonfiction is, in other words, primarily utilitarian—useful for some practical purpose.

Poetry and imaginative prose as well have other goals and effects in mind. Poetry gives one not just an *idea* about something but creates within the skillful reader its shape and human feel. It takes the reader vicariously into the life of other people—the writer or the writer's imagined characters. What is it like to *be* an independent but deeply committed Christian in the seventeenth century? Read John Milton's *Paradise Lost*. What does it feel like to see God as holy and righteous and yourself as a sinner who cannot get free of his own sin? Read John Donne's prayer in Holy Sonnet 14: "Batter My Heart."

In the next section we will indeed do this. We will look

briefly at a number of short poems which have over the past thirty years meant a great deal to me. I will try to capture their shape and illuminate their appeal. Then a long section will be devoted to the close analysis of one poem which has a fairly simple meaning on the level of ideas but a very deep meaning on the level of art. The chapter will close by discussing the place of world views in understanding poetry.

In all of this I hope to convince those readers who are reluctant to give poetry the time of day that good poetry is worth the time of many days and many nights too. To readers who already love poetry I hope to offer a few more insights to understanding this rich medium of expression. In any case, what I write in this entire chapter is not meant to be primarily a key to understanding a few poems but rather a set of tools to use in understanding all the poetry you read.

Catching Reality in a Mirror

About the great events of life prose seems an inadequate means of expression. Love, death, fate, the capture of a city, the defeat of an archenemy: to reflect on these with depth is to engage, if only internally, in a poetic monolog. Whenever one feels deeply, whenever mere words seem inadequate to capture the quality of a moment or an idea, we turn to poetry, either by writing it or searching for the right poem to read and meditate on.

What is the primary reason for reading poetry or any imaginative literature? Beyond all psychologizing as to real or apparent motives, we read literature because we enjoy it—and we enjoy it because we are grabbed by it, our attention is arrested. We say, "Aha! Yes, *that's* how it is."

In great literature—poetry and fiction—we see ourselves, our friends, our enemies, the world around us. We see our interests portrayed in bold relief—our questions asked better than we can ask them, our problems pictured better than we can picture them by ourselves, our fantasies realized beyond our fondest dreams, our fears confirmed in horrors more horrible than our nightmares, our hopes fulfilled past our ability to yearn or desire.

In literature we catch reality in a mirror. We are not seeing life raw—all spread out in a flux which we have to bring to order. We are seeing, at least in the greatest literature, life structured, chaos ordered, the flux halted, the transient nailed down. In literature we can pass the same way twice, have the same experience over and over again, each time intensified.

Life, our life, is short, but art is long. Sophocles is dead, but Oedipus lives on and on, and is recreated hundreds of thousands of times as generation after generation brings him to life by reading *Oedipus Rex* or seeing it performed on stage. Each of us when we read a great piece of literature is a little more human than before, a little more able to say with meaning, "This, then, is man."

I have long been a lover of poetry. I remember enjoying Shakespeare in high school as our patient English teacher took us line by line through a series of his plays. But it was not until college that certain poems began to stick with me. I couldn't get them out of my mind.

Emily Dickinson's brief lyric poem is chief among those indelibly printed on my memory:

After great pain, a formal feeling comes.
The nerves sit ceremonious, like tombs.
The stiff heart questions was it He that bore,
And yesterday, or centuries before?

The feet, mechanical, go round
A wooden way
Of ground, or air, or ought

Regardless grown,
A quartz contentment, like a stone.

This is the hour of lead
Remembered if outlived,
As freezing persons recollect the snow,
First the chill, then the stupor and then the letting go.[1]

Throughout the years often when I've been tired and emo-
tionally down the words come to me: "This is the hour of
lead." And then the last line: "First the chill, then the stupor
and then the letting go."

Of course, Emily Dickinson was not just talking about
being down at the mouth. She was capturing in words and
images the feeling that comes "after great pain," probably
the specific pain one feels after the death of a close friend.
Do you see how she catches the stiffness of the affair? The
nerves are overloaded, the emotions don't work, the body
tenses—"a formal feeling comes," the feeling of a funeral.
Even "the nerves sit ceremonious like tombs." And the
hardened heart that beats its muted beat asks its awful questions: What happened? Why? Did not Christ bear our in-
firmities centuries before? Then what was the meaning of
the one who died yesterday?

Everything in the immediate aftermath of death turns
cold and wooden. And the griever moves mechanically
through the hours of preparation for the ceremonies of
death. Indeed "this *is* the hour of lead," barely, if at all,
remembered. The poet then summons up the final image
of freezing persons. Do they ever recollect the snow? No.
First it's "the chill, then the stupor, then the letting go," as
one slips into oblivion. Or is it perhaps that the dammed-up
emotions are released and the mourner again becomes a
human being, the stiffness gone, the heart resilient, the life
restored? We cannot escape the ambiguity: perhaps both

are intended.

What makes this poem work such magic in our minds? It is not the depth of thought. Surely that is common enough. It is not even the depth of feeling. Rather it is the power of the poem to evoke in the reader memories of death, to call these to account in the form of words in carefully crafted lines. The emotions here have not been allowed to be sentimental—to be inappropriate to the event and its human meanings. Rather they are caught on the fly, made to behave, made to fit into the larger pattern of human experience. These are the ways of grief. These are its verbal coordinates. This is how it is.

The primary power of the poem comes from the images, and the careful reader of this particular poem will probably not spend so much time counting syllables or checking rhyme schemes or sentence structure as in contemplating the images themselves and the words used to cast them on the screen of imagination. Note a few: *the hour of lead,* the *nerves* that *sit ceremonious* (how? *like tombs*), *the stiff heart,* the *quartz contentment* and so forth.

How do these images make you feel? Emily Dickinson once wrote, "If I read a book and it makes my whole body so cold no fire can ever warm me, I know *that* is poetry. If I feel physically as if the top of my head were taken off, I know *that* is poetry. These are the only ways I know it. Is there any other way?" This feeling is, indeed, not an accurate criterion for all poetry, but it does help us understand that Dickinson was well aware of the emotional—even sensuous—quality of poetry.

Is it all feeling? No. There is questioning too. In the face of this death what is the meaning of the death of Christ? No cheap answer is given. No sentimental silver lining shines behind this cloud. There are no clouds—just the clanking of the human machine as it goes through the motions of life.

What a contrast to this is Gerard Manley Hopkins's beautiful sonnet "Hurrahing in Harvest." Here it is not death that is mourned but life that is celebrated. This is a somewhat more complicated poem to grasp at first reading. But no poem worth reading is worth reading only once, or twice or.... So let's get on with it:

> Summer ends now; now, barbarous in beauty, the stooks
>   rise
> Around; up above, what wind-walks! what lovely
>   behaviour
> Of silk-sack clouds! has wilder, wilful-wavier
> Meal-drift moulded ever and melted across skies?
>
> I walk, I lift up, I lift up heart, eyes,
> Down all that glory in the heavens to glean our Saviour;
> And, eyes, heart, what looks, what lips yet gave you a
> Rapturous love's greeting of realer, of rounder replies?
>
> And the azurous hung hills are his world-wielding
>   shoulder
> Majestic—as a stallion stalwart, very-violet-sweet!—
> These things, these things were here and but the
>   beholder
> Wanting; which two when they once meet,
> The heart rears wings bold and bolder
> And hurls for him, O half hurls earth for him off under
>   his feet.[2]

Baffled? Okay. Re-read it and then pick up with the next paragraph.

Are you familiar with what is there in the poem? If not, read it again and then drop to the next paragraph.

Okay. I'm finished playing with you. At least I didn't ask you to do what one author did in the first sentence of a book: "Close your eyes tightly."

What is the scene the poet is showing us? The time is the end of summer, the scene is a field of ripened and shocked grain that is "barbarous in beauty." The stooks, the shocks of grain, rise around him, and above him the silk-sack clouds walk with the wind. The sky is awhirl with action.

"Has this ever happened before?" asks Hopkins the poet in wonderment. And looking for the reasons for such vitality in the autumn scene, he finds it in the Savior himself. The poet walks and, lifting up his heart and eyes and playing them across all the glory he sees around him, he gleans the Savior as the harvesters have gleaned the fields. There the distant hills are the very shoulders of our Lord—majestic, sweet.

Reveling in the revelation of God's Spirit in autumn (shades of Ps. 19:1-6), he turns inward and comments on his own part in the joy. He asks his eyes and heart, if any other person ("looks and lips") has greeted him with a more rapturous, more real reply than has our Savior through this autumn scene. For this experience two things must be present: the majesty of autumn and the beholder. When this happens a person's heart "rears wings" and almost bears him off with the clouds, that is, "half hurls earth for him off under his feet."

I hesitate to ask this again, but would you now return to page 62 and read the poem yet once more. This time read it aloud. Poetry is meant to be read aloud. "Listen" to it.

Do you feel it working on you? Give yourself to its sounds. Surely in this poem sounds are more important than in "After Great Pain." For here are the windy sounds of *w*'s and *m*'s in the first four lines, the liquid sounds of *l*'s, *g*'s and *r*'s in the second four lines and the hefty, weight-hurling sounds of *h*'s in the last two lines. Let your tongue play lightly over these and other repeated sounds. They are not gratuitous. You are experiencing the magic of language controlled by a master. And all is to this end—to elicit in you the reader a response to God's created world that is appropriate to God-created people.

What a difference there is between deeply reading a great, though tiny, work like this sonnet and skipping from poem to poem like an American tourist dashing from sculpture to painting, seeing Europe through the eyes of guidebook prose: "This mosaic is constructed of 750,000 individual pieces [the number is always large beyond comprehension] and took 36,000 hours to complete." To see the work of an artist like this is not even to see through a glass darkly.

What else makes this poem work so profoundly on us? Well, syntax certainly plays an important role. Repeated syntactical structures heighten the drama: "I walk, I lift up, I lift up heart, eyes." And then the twist: I lift *up* heart and eyes, but I do so *down* all the glory in the sky. Scan the poem with just this idea in mind and see how many parallelisms and twists you find, as, for example, in lines 7 and 8 or 11 and 14.

In a Hopkins poem rhythm and rhyme, phrases which run around lines, and sentences which stop in the middle of lines all play a key role. We could dwell at great length on them here. But let us look at a few more poems briefly before reading any single poem in depth.

The Simple and the Profound
Both Emily Dickinson's and Gerard Manley Hopkins's poems are well-crafted works of art. Sometimes seemingly very simple poems have an almost equally profound effect. One of my college professors would often quote a four-line verse that apparently moved him deeply.

    Yesterday upon the stair,

I met a man who wasn't there.
I met him there again today.
God, I wish he'd go away.

I do not know the origin of this nursery-rhyme takeoff. I don't think my professor did either. But after slowly quoting it deliberately and line by line, he would say, "That frightens me. That frightens me."

It has never really frightened me, but it has my children. One day when I had been remembering these lines, I tried them out on my family.

I knew the last line might be a bit inappropriate for the children and so I said,

Yesterday upon the stair,
I met a man who wasn't there.
I met him there again today.
Gee, I wish he'd go away.

I believe it was Gene, then about eight years old who looked up at me, as Keats might say, in "a wild surmise," and said excitedly, "Who was it, Daddy? Was it God? Was it Jesus?"

Indeed, who is the "man who wasn't there"? Somehow this little lyric drops down the shaft of consciousness into the pool of the subliminal and all sorts of ghosts fly up. Which of us has not met some ghost of himself, some being from beyond or below, there on the stairway in the morning as we descend from the realm of night and emerge into the waking light of day? Doppelgängers, demigods, entities of the dark haunt the shadow lands of our consciousness. This poem brings to awareness in our fully waking mind the memory of those misty midregions of our not-too-well-known souls.

In other words, the power of this poem comes from its

"mythic" quality. It stays with us in part because of that but
also because its simple form with simple words is easily remembered. Mother Goose has never been so black, but perhaps never more memorable either.

Alfred Lord Tennyson's lyric "The Eagle" is also a seemingly simple poem. Like "Yesterday upon the Stair" it
strikes a chord deep inside. Question: Is the poem about an
eagle or something else, say, something characteristic about
humankind?

> He clasps the crag with crooked hands:
> Close to the sun in lonely lands.
> Ringed with the azure world, he stands.
>
> The wrinkled sea beneath him crawls:
> He watches from his mountain walls.
> And like a thunderbolt he falls.

Notice first the double perspective. Stanza 1 is a view seen
from below: the eagle is way up above "close to the sun" and
"ringed" with the sky. Stanza 2 is a view from above: the sea
is way down below, so far below that the waves are wrinkles.
In poems like this and, say, "Hurrahing in Harvest" it is
vitally important to *see* these word pictures with the mind's
eye. Read the poem again just to do that.

Then notice the anthropomorphic language used to describe the eagle and his actions. He has *hands* (not *claws*); he
stands (not *perches*). Even the inanimate ocean is given
characteristics of animate life: it *crawls* (rather than *undu-
lates*).

In the poem the eagle, however, is the only being that is
alive. And that is explicitly pointed out: he stands "close
to the sun in *lonely* lands." Is there not, however, another
being hinted at in the poem? What is the eagle looking for
from his mountain walls? Why does he fall "like a thunder-

bolt"? Is it not that he is pouncing on a prey? So here, then, emerges the picture of a lonely eagle whose only desire is to act out his craggy eagleness in destroying one life so he may live. Have we read too much into the poem? Is this all intended by Lord Tennyson? Of course, we will never know how much Tennyson's poem is modified by our own vision. We do know that his poem has been read by thousands of people for over a hundred years and is continually anthologized in collections of poetry. Why? Indeed it is a striking picture of an eagle. But why so striking? Perhaps because we see our lonely selves somewhere in the picture alongside, even within, the bird with crooked hands so much like ours. As we noted earlier, poetry is multilinear. It can mean and is often intended to mean many things. On one level it is the picture story of an eagle, on another a read-out of human character.

Sometimes the magic of a poem will almost completely escape understanding. I for one have never grasped why William Carlos Williams's poem, "The Red Wheelbarrow," has such an effect on me.

So much depends
upon

a red wheel
barrow

glazed with rain
water

beside the white
chickens

At first it looks like just a word picture—an image—red wheelbarrow, glazed with rainwater, beside white chickens.

What's so special about that? Yet Williams says, "So much depends" precisely on that. And it is this simple proposition that lifts the image into art. It makes us ask why, and though it does not answer the question, it arrests our attention and directs it to something aesthetically beautiful and pleasing that otherwise we might not have seen at all. There is a beauty and a value to the ordinary objects of life. We should notice, too, something about the form of the lines themselves. At first they may look haphazard, formless. But look again. Here are four two-line units; in each unit the first line has three words, the second line has one. There is obviously more form here than we might first imagine. But there is something more striking: what does each of these lines look like simply considered as visual form? In other words, how many wheelbarrows are pictured in the poem?

Williams's poem is like a still-life painting. Quality presents itself quietly and yet persistently. And, though we cannot say why we see, we see.

I have taken time to discuss briefly a few specific poems for several reasons. First, I have wanted those with an antipathy to poetry to see that some poems offer real joy without demanding much from the reader. Poetry is not always so obscure that it yields its treasure only to professional students of the art.

Second, I have hoped to show that even simple poems have a widely divergent character. They do not all succeed for the same reasons. Some depend more on image, others on verbal gymnastics, still others on triggering subliminal psychological responses. Poems in tone and temper, shape and feel, form and content, can be as different from each other as the views of B. F. Skinner are from those of C. S. Lewis.

Our task (and in terms of effort it is a task) is to learn to read well enough so that we can see what is really there to see. Reading nonfiction prose well rewards us by helping us understand the context of ideas common to humanity. Reading poetry and other imaginative literature rewards us by helping us experience vicariously not only the way other people think but also the way they feel as they think. To read poetry well is to become more fully human, not because poetry inevitably leads us to truth about reality but because it forges a bond of human sympathy with those not like ourselves whom we come to see as if they were ourselves. We learn to see with the eyes and heart and mind of others—certainly a goal worth striving for.

Of Skyscrapers and Poems
There are, I suppose, many ways to learn to read poetry well. The method I will explain here is based on my own background as a reader, of course, but also on the work of such scholars and critics as Samuel Taylor Coleridge, Cleanth Brooks, Robert Penn Warren and John Ciardi. I could hardly recommend a more helpful book, for example, than Ciardi's *How Does a Poem Mean?*[3] In the section that follows the present one I will depart rather radically from the techniques of the so-called New Critics. But here for the purpose of reading poetry as poetry I am much in their debt.

The assumption on which the following suggestions for reading are based is this: every genuine poem is a linguistic structure composed of overlapping (amplifying/tension-producing) substructures unified by some principle (some form or conception).

This is, of course, a *formal* definition of a poem. It sounds cold and abstract. I suspect that it doesn't even look as if it makes sense. I will grant that appearance at the moment, but hear me out.

First, a poem is a *linguistic structure*. That is a fancy way to say that a poem is composed of words arranged in one specific way and no other. The words of each poem have a structure peculiar to them. So the question is, In any given poem what is that structure?

Every poem has not just a single overall structure but many substructures as well. Think of a large skyscraper. It has an overall form which we can see from miles around, but it is not just one thing; it is a unity of many. Its height is a function of, say, one hundred and three stories piled one on another. Its outer shell is glass and marble, its interior frame steel and concrete in carefully crafted form, beams tied to beams in such a way as to support the towering building. Then too there is an electrical substructure providing light and power to each room. There is a scheme of rooms and hallways, elevator shafts, ventilator shafts and stairways. There is a water system, an air-conditioning system, a phone system. And each of these has a substructure of its own—wires, tubes, bolts, rivets. The skyscraper would be incomplete with any of its substructures missing.

So a poem, though not so awesome, is a structure—not of physical materials but of words. A poem is a linguistic structure.

To understand a building, we examine it closely, go to the blueprint to see, as it were, behind the walls. To understand a poem we do the same thing. And just as architects or building engineers know what to look for when they examine the building, so do good readers. What, then, are the substructures of a poem?

The way we will view a poem is to see it as a unity of the following substructures: (1) paraphrasable content, (2) rational structure, (3) image structure, (4) metrical structure, (5) sound structure and (6) syntactical structure. If we examine a poem for these elementary structures, we will come to see it for what it is and thus be able to experience it more fully. At least, that will be our attempt in the pages that follow.

To give our analysis concrete substance we will focus our attention on William Shakespeare's Sonnet 73. Here is the poem itself:

> That time of year thou mayst in me behold
> When yellow leaves, or none, or few, do hang
> Upon those boughs which shake against the cold,
> Bare ruin'd choirs, where late the sweet birds sang.
> In me thou see'st the twilight of such day
> As after sunset fadeth in the west,
> Which by and by black night doth take away,
> Death's second self, that seals up all in rest.
> In me thou see'st the glowing of such fire
> That on the ashes of his youth doth lie,
> As the death-bed whereon it must expire
> Consumed with that which it was nourish'd by.
> This thou perceivest, which makes thy love more
>   strong,
> To love that well which thou must leave ere long.

Paraphrasable content. Our first task is to get an overall sense of the poem. Who is speaking the lines? To whom are they spoken? What is the subject? What, basically, is being said about that subject? In other words, what is the paraphrasable content?

Re-read the poem to answer those questions. This is not a difficult or obscure poem and the answers are not hard to find.

The "poet" (or speaker of the lines) is directly addressing another person ("thou," line 1). The subject is the poet's death imagined to take place soon. A simple summary (or paraphrase) of what the poet says to his friend is this: *You*

may now look at me and see that, like autumn, like twilight and like
the dying of a fire, I will soon be gone; in seeing this, you will love
me more because you will soon be leaving me.

Because this is the simple core idea of the poem, some
readers may be tempted to say, "Oh, I see. So that's what the
poem means. Well, why didn't the poet say so instead of
taking so long and being so all-fired artsy-craftsy about it?"

There are two things to say in response. For one thing,
this paraphrase is not the *meaning* of the poem; it is only
the core idea. For another thing, the speaker of the poem
did not intend only to send this core idea as a message
to his friend. To have done this would not have represented
what he really wished to say. He wanted to "say" the whole
poem. And he wanted us as readers to overhear him as
he addresses his friend. His poem has a meaning for us as
well.

Still, let's not play down the significance of the core idea.
It is the unifying intellectual thread that ties together the
fourteen lines. There are other unifying elements, but in
our attempt to see all the substructures in the poem we must
not overlook this important one. As Nathan A. Scott, Jr.
has said, it is easy to neglect "the incorrigibly referential
thrust that words do have. . . . They insist on pointing to
things."[4] The words in Shakespeare's poem are not just
colors daubed on canvas with only a formal relation to each
other. There is an idea that is being expressed and conveyed: the poet sees himself growing older and he points
out to his friend that his love will, perhaps must, intensify
as he recognizes this is happening.

Rational structure. Closely related to the paraphrasable
content is the rational structure. The paraphrasable content of a poem is the idea (or ideas) of the poem; *the rational*
structure is the order in which the ideas are expressed.

In literary works time is a factor. One does not grasp a

poem as one might grasp a painting—all at once in a single vision. At least a reader does not do this without first going through a time-qualified process. In poetry some things come before others. In this observation of the obvious lies the key to the notion of rational structure. A good reader will notice the orderliness (indeed, the specific order in which the ideas come).

What, then, is the order of ideas in Sonnet 73? Re-read the poem with that question in mind.

Again the answer is simple. In lines 1-4 the poet says: In me you see autumn. In lines 5-8 he says: In me you see twilight. In lines 9-12 he says: In me you see the dying of the fires of life. Finally in lines 13-14, he applies these perceptions to his friend's attitude to him. It's a sort of argument along the lines of *because* so and so is the case, *therefore* such and such follows. The rational structure expressed in numbers of lines is: 4-4-4-2. This may mean nothing to us now, but we will certainly see its significance later.

It is, of course, possible to break down the internal rational structure of each of the four lines, but, in this case, not too much will be accomplished. As we will see later, there is a syntactical (sentence-structural) reason for this.

We should also note that there is no set style for rational structure in a poem. Not all sonnets have the same arrangement, not all of Shakespeare's sonnets, perhaps not another single one. We could find out only by analyzing all one hundred and fifty-four of them. The good reader does not begin by finding what he is looking for, but by finding what is there. Observation is the key to good reading.

Image structure. In this particular poem, the image structure is so closely related to the rational structure that we have already talked about it without saying so. There are three major images, each depicting imminent death: autumn (lines 1-4), evening (lines 5-8) and the dying fire (lines 9-12). The final two lines are imageless; that is they are a flat prosaic statement. So here is that same pattern we saw above: 4-4-4-(2), the parenthesis indicating the absence of imagery.

The order is easy to perceive, but something further about that order will be obvious if we look closely. Is there a principle discernible in the order itself? That is, is there any reason why autumn comes before twilight or twilight before the dying fire? Why didn't Shakespeare begin with the dying fire?

One might say, "Well, one of them has to come first. Does it make any difference?" Perhaps not. But let's look again. There is one factor about each image that we have not yet noted: duration. Autumn takes, say, three months; twilight a few hours; a dying fire perhaps only a few minutes. Now we see the reason. Each time the friend is said to see the poet's dying as a more and more immediate possibility. And so the conclusion is strengthened. Death is rushing faster and faster to meet his friend; thus his love is intensified all the more.

Try re-reading the poem with the sequence in mind and see if the intensity is not reflected and even summoned up in your own imagination. To have reversed the order of images would have been to confuse the emotional order, to have dissipated its intensity rather than heightened it.

Metrical structure. We turn now to a structure which takes a bit more time to see and appreciate. With this structure we leave the tourist group and get down with the engineers to pore over the blueprint for the skyscraper.

The metrical structure is simply the pattern of stressed and unstressed syllables in the poem. Most readers of this book will at least have heard the term *iambic pentameter,* and many will know what it means. But for those who don't, I will begin at the beginning.

Every sentence of the English language has some stressed (accented) and some unstressed (unaccented) syllables. The way in which these stressed and unstressed syllables are ordered is called *rhythm*.

Poetry is not unique in having rhythm. Rather, poetry just pays special attention to this rhythm, makes it into a pattern with the express purpose not only of giving form to the lines but of giving that *specific* form which will most enhance the intended effect of the whole.

Let's take an example from Sonnet 73. Read line 1 and note the stressed (/) and the unstressed (x) syllables:

$$\overset{x}{\text{That}} \overset{/}{\text{time}} \overset{x}{\text{of}} \overset{/}{\text{year}} \overset{x}{\text{thou}} \overset{/}{\text{mayst}} \overset{x}{\text{in}} \overset{/}{\text{me}} \overset{x}{\text{be}}\overset{/}{\text{hold}}$$

It is, of course, possible to give a dramatic reading of the lines and place a stress on *That* or *thou*. But unless we are being affected or humorous, we will not stress *of* or *in* or the first syllable of *behold*. In other words there is nothing magic about determining which syllables are stressed and which are not. The stress we are looking at here is the one we discover when we reflect on what we do when we read naturally.

Now let us look at what we have found in this line: ten syllables with alternating unstressed and stressed syllables. This can be seen as five equal two-syllable units (x /). In metrical terminology each of these units (x /) is called an *iamb*. When five such units are found in one line, the line is called an *iambic pentameter* line. Terms are not so important, however, as the observation and the "feel" for the pattern itself as we read. Of course there are many other possible patterns which we will examine later.

We should now see whether the remainder of the poem keeps up this basic iambic pattern. And so to line 2:

$$\overset{x}{\text{When}} \overset{/}{\text{yellow}} \overset{x}{\text{leaves,}} \overset{/}{\text{or}} \overset{x}{\text{none,}} \overset{/}{\text{or}} \overset{x}{\text{few,}} \overset{/}{\text{do}} \overset{x}{\text{hang}}$$

Indeed the pattern is the same. What about line 3?

    x /   x   /   x   /   x /   x   /
Upon those boughs which shake against the cold,

Again we could stress *those;* that would be an option for a
reader trying to capture a nuance. The iambic pentameter
pattern is still very much with us. But isn't that what we
learned in high school or maybe grade school? Didn't the
teacher say, "Shakespeare wrote in iambic pentameter"?
Seems as if we must have checked that on a dozen multiple-
choice tests. So what's new?

Well, line 4, for one thing:

   /   / x /   x /   x /   /   /
Bare ruin'd choirs, where late the sweet birds sang.

Suddenly, we have found a break in the pattern. It is just
not possible to speak the English language properly and not
stress *bare* and *ruin'd* and *choirs.* Try reading the line in
iambic stress and see what happens.

   x / x   /   x /   x /   x   /
Bare ruin'd choirs, where late the sweet birds sang.

We notice that two words which we naturally stress are not
stressed (*bare* and *birds*). So how does Shakespeare wish us to
read the line? Here is an important principle: always read a
line of poetry the way you would read a line of prose, giving
the syllables the stress that seems most natural to the flow
of the sentence. Shakespeare in line 4 has not written
iambic pentameter.

It is important to ask why Shakespeare chose to alter a
pattern established in the first three lines. That is what we
will try eventually to discover. I think at least one answer
will become plain when we have looked at the total pattern
of the fourteen lines.

The second set of four lines we will see as a unit, now that
we have begun to get the hang of locating stressed and unstressed syllables:

In me thou see'st the twilight of such day
As after sunset fadeth in the west,
Which by and by black night doth take away,
Death's second self, that seals up all in rest.

These lines obviously contain further variations from the iambic pattern. Though in a dramatic reading some might stress *thou* (line 5) or *doth* (line 7), few readers will pronounce *twilight* or *sunset* (line 6) with an unstressed syllable and none will be able to keep from accenting *Death's* (line 8). The irregularities, from the standpoint of iambic pentameter, are plain. Again, we wish to ask why, but we need to see the metrical structure of the whole poem before we can answer.

The third set of four lines (called a *quatrain* in poetic terminology) can be scanned for stress as follows:

In me thou see'st the glowing of such fire
That on the ashes of his youth doth lie,
As the death-bed whereon it must expire
Consumed with that which it was nourish'd by.

Line 9 contains only one variation at the end, and line 12 is regular. But lines 10 and 11 are very odd by comparison. Since we now have so many variations to account for, it may be helpful to introduce further metrical terms.

The first *foot* (metrical unit, composed of two syllables in this instance) of line 10 is composed of two unstressed syllables (x x). This kind of foot is called *pyrrhic*. The last foot of line 10 is composed of two stressed syllables (/ /). This kind of foot is called a *spondee*. The only possible variation of stress remaining for a two-syllable foot is a stressed syllable followed by an unstressed syllable (/ x) and that is called a *trochee.* Depending on how we wish to read line 13, we might say it begins with a trochee.

This thou perceivest, which makes thy love more strong,
To love that well which thou must leave ere long.

We could read line 13 as beginning with a spondee and even ending with a spondee. That would cast an emphasis on *thou* and *more,* but we cannot rid our reading of a stress on *This.* Note, too, that for line 13 to contain only ten syllables, *perceivest* must be read as two syllables.

But there is something interesting here. Suddenly we discover that the last three lines of the poem are almost regular again. Only the opening of line 13 keeps these three lines from returning to the completely iambic pentameter rhythm of the first three lines. There is thus a symmetry to the metrical structure. That can be our first observation helpful in determining why there are variations elsewhere. Shakespeare has laid down a basic pattern. There is no question that the overall rhythm is iambic pentameter. He has begun with it and ended with it.

The variations, therefore, must be there to call attention to something. To what? Let's make a list of the variations noting the places where stresses (which almost always suggest emphasis) fall together: *Bare ru(in'd)* (line 4), *sweet birds sang* (line 4), *twilight* (line 5), *such day* (line 5), *sunset fad(eth)* (line 6), *by black night* (line 7), *death's sec(ond)* (line 8), *such fire* (line 9), *doth lie* (line 10), *death-bed* (line 11) and perhaps *more strong* (line 13).

Though it may not seem obvious at first, upon reflection several reasons for these combinations of stressed syllables emerge. First, in line 4, the two variations occur on each end of the line. But notice as well that the ideas expressed by the stressed words are opposite: *Bare ru(in'd)* versus *sweet birds sang.* The spondees point up the contrast.

Second, the spondees in lines 5-8 all fall on words related to light, either fading light or total darkness. Thus the image of nightfall is brought more sharply into our consciousness, though until we see this metrical machinery exposed, it is all completely below our level of awareness. Good reading brings this "formal meaning" to consciousness.

Third, the spondees in lines 9-12 emphasize lying on a death-bed, and even the one outstanding stressed word of line 10, *ash(es),* highlights the power of the metaphor.

Finally, line 13, like line 4, read with as much stress as is natural, balances two spondees:

This thou perceivest, which makes thy love more strong,

The first spondee arrests our attention after a regular iambic line, and the last highlights the implications of the argument. Indeed, the friend's love must be *more* strong. The final line then peacefully returns to the regular rhythm and a sense of harmony is conveyed.

In sum, the metrical structure of the poem reinforces its images and its content. In this case, no new meaning is added. But the poem as a whole is made more powerful because all its parts work together.

There is no telling what we may find when we look closely at any aspect of a poem, and that is especially true of the metrical structure. For metrical structure is not something to which we give any conscious attention in daily discourse. Of course, in speech and ordinary prose we do make rhythm work for us. And the better speakers and writers we are the more we are likely to know what we are doing with rhythm. Still, a careful attention to metrics does not come with mother's milk; we need to develop it. Try a metrical analysis on a piece of writing—prose or poetry—that you find powerful. You might be surprised to learn how much of the power derives from its rhythm.

Sound structure. For some unskilled readers rhyme is the only really "poetic" thing about poetry. If a bunch of lines rhyme, they are poetry. If a bunch of lines don't rhyme, they aren't poetry. But this surely is wrong on both counts. Rhyme does not make poetry out of a group of otherwise undistinguished lines; nor does every legitimate poem rhyme. Blank verse, the metrical line most used by Shakespeare and Milton, is defined as "unrhymed iambic pentameter." So: poetry need not rhyme.

But much poetry does. And if it does, that pattern of rhyme is an important, perhaps the most important, aspect of a poem's sound structure. Clearly this sonnet by Shakespeare rhymes. So, what is its structure?

Looking back over the first four lines of the poem, we find that the first and third lines rhyme and the second and fourth lines rhyme. Symbolically that is usually expressed: *abab,* each letter representing the kind of sound ending each line. Using that system throughout the poem gives us the following: *ababcdcdefefgg.*

In other words, in terms of rhyme we have *a* and *b* interlocking to form the first quatrain, *c* and *d* forming the second quatrain, *e* and *f* the third, and *g* doubling to form the final couplet. This is a 4-4-4-2 pattern which overlaps precisely the image structures and rational structures of the poem—one quatrain per sound unit, one quatrain per image unit, one quatrain per rational unit, for three quatrains; then the couplet rounds it off, or closes off the form, like a lid on a jewel box clicking shut. The couplet says in rhyme, in rational content and even in lack of imagery (the other 4-line units all have a dominant image) that the poem is finished.

Not every sonnet has this same rhyme scheme. All of Shakespeare's sonnets do, and that's why the *ababcdcdefefgg* form is called a Shakespearean sonnet. Many sonnets, by Shakespeare's contemporaries as well as by Milton, Wordsworth and Keats, have a scheme laid down on an 8-6 division of the 14 lines: for example, *abbaabbacdcdcd*. The *a* rhyme begins and closes the first eight lines making it a unit; the *cd* links the last six lines. Other variations on the final 6 lines are *cdcdee* (another 4-2 division) and *cdecde* (a 3-3 division).

Again, I want to emphasize that good readers will not force a poem to fit their own expectations. (Poets know what readers expect and often deliberately try to surprise them.) Good readers observe what is there and then, one hopes, begin to see how what is there contributes to the overall effect.

Sound structure in poetry is not limited to rhyme. Any systematic or repeated use of similar sounds is a part of the sound structure of the poem. For example, the final line of Shakespeare's sonnet contains some obvious repetition:

To *l*ove that we*ll* which thou must *l*eave ere *l*ong.

This repetition of consonant sounds is called *alliteration*. There is also some alliteration of the *s* sound in lines 4-6, 8-9 and 13. Some poems contain a great deal of alliteration. Shakespeare and Spenser used it extensively and Gerard Manley Hopkins was in love with it; we have already noticed the alliteration in "Hurrahing in Harvest." Poets also use *assonance* ("the close repetition of similar vowel sounds, usually in stressed syllables") and *cacophony* ("discordant or harsh sound") in order to achieve a good relationship between sound and sense.[5]

The question for the reader is, What do these verbal gymnastics do for the poem? First, of course, they call attention to the special way the language is being used. Most prose and most ordinary speech are undistinguished by special verbal effects. Only when the orator gets to a high point in his speech does he call on alliteration and other rhetorical gimmicks to get his audience to pay special attention. In other words, when the sound of language calls attention to itself, it means the poet wants the reader to pay attention.

Second, the special effects of sound are qualified by their surrounding context of form and content—other sound effects (or lack of them) and the ideas being discussed. In regard to form we can notice, for example, that only the alliteration in line 14 is striking and only here is the *l* sound so obviously repeated. Note also that this is the last line in the poem. Is the poet saying by this formal device, "You see, dear reader, the poem is over"? In content, we can note that the softness of the *l* sound supports the positive notion of love, a topic which is first introduced directly only in the couplet. Is Shakespeare contrasting the otherwise grim aspects of death and the pain of separation not only by idea but by sound as well (the harsh *death's second self* as contrasted with the mellifluous *love* and *leave ere long*)? We can only speculate, but surely we can hear and feel the positive flow of the last line as contrasted with the negative feel of lines 9-12.

As we read well-written prose and poetry and begin to pay attention to sounds, we will also begin to pay attention to sense and thus come away from our reading with more than mere ideas.

Syntactical structure. Every sentence has a specific arrangement of words, a specific grammatical structure. The most common English sentence begins with its subject and proceeds to its predicate: for example, *John* (subject) *threw the ball* (predicate). Here the predicate can be further di-

vided into *threw* (verb) and *the ball* (direct object).
All of this is or was once well known to all readers of this
book, as are many other variations, deviations and developments of English syntax. But very few of us think about how
we structure our sentences. As native users of English our
sophistication with the language (or lack of it) is unstudied,
unconscious. When we read poetry, however, we can often
learn something about why a poem is effective (or ineffec-
tive) by looking at the sentence structure of its various lines.
Let's turn again to Shakespeare's Sonnet 73. How many
sentences are there? Immediately we see the pattern: there
are four sentences of 4, 4, 4 and 2 lines respectively. Sentence structure is now seen to coincide with and thus rein-
force rational structure, image structure and rhyme structure.

Do we find any repeated grammatical patterns? Indeed,
the second and third quatrains both begin *in me thou see'st*.
Obviously this repetition serves to enforce the parallelism
of idea between the two quatrains.

Are there any unusual sentence patterns or grammatical
forms within the individual sentences? To fully answer this
question would take us many pages, but we can make some
simple observations. First, the opening sentence inverts the
normal English pattern of subject-verb-object: *That time of
year* (object) *thou* (subject) *mayst in me behold* (verb). Generally, when the object is placed first in a sentence, special
attention is called to it. Indeed, that is appropriate here, for
the whole sonnet is about time—the effect of time on the
relationship between the speaker of the poem and the one
he is addressing.

The final sentence of the poem also inverts the normal
order: *This* (object) *thou* (subject) *perceivest* (verb). The break
between the first twelve lines and the last two is thus emphasized, and again we are reminded that the final couplet

is indeed the couplet which is *final*.

Further grammatical analysis would undoubtedly yield more insight into the ways this poem works. We could note, for example, that not all the lines of the poem end with a grammatical pause. Lines 2, 3 and 4 should be read continuously; thus sentence structure governs the rhythm of reading. Many other such observations could be made. But it is time to return to the whole poem.

The Whole Poem

After poring over blueprints with the architect, we may feel that we have lost sight of the overall form and function of the skyscraper. Yes, we may feel that way at first. But now we know the building from the inside out. After all, it really does have an electrical system, a heating system, a water system and so forth. Most of this structure is hidden, but if it weren't there the skyscraper would no longer function.

Now as we pull away from our detailed analysis and hold it in the back of our minds, as it were, we are ready again to see the poem as a whole. Try reading it just reflecting on what it is doing to you at the moment you read. You will no longer be able to read it without being conscious of its inner workings, and you will, I believe, be able to experience the poem and "understand" it much more fully than before.

So now we can ask again, this time with more depth, What does the poem mean? And we can answer: it *means* its paraphrasable content plus all of the qualification and enhancement conveyed by the impact of sound, imagery, rational structure and syntax. As we read Sonnet 73 we should now be "feeling" vicariously with the poet something of the impact that the passage of time has on human relationships. People die, they leave behind their friends, their wives and husbands, their lovers. To see that, to feel time—yes, death—creep up, first like autumn, then like twilight and finally like the last glowing but dimming coal of an old fire is to become a little more human than before.

Actually, the affirmation of life—of love and human value in the face of death—in Sonnet 73 is general enough to be accepted as true by most naturalists as well as by most Christians. Shakespeare here has given us little clue to his larger view of human nature. We cannot tell from this poem alone whether he sees human beings as created in the image of God or as a product of impersonal natural forces, whether he sees us as basically good or totally depraved. We would need to read other sonnets and perhaps some plays to glean his more extensive world view. Most lyric poems, because they are short, will only display a portion of any poet's world view. In the case of Sonnet 73, however, we will find as Christians many sympathetic vibrations.

And so Sonnet 73 when drunk to the full becomes a link in the chain of our inner biography. To the extent that its perception of life is true, we are the better for it.

A Window on Other Worlds
There is certainly no guarantee that any given poem will "tell the truth" or help us "experience" a particular piece of the truth. What if the skyscraper should turn out to be a temple to Baal or a brothel in Soho? Poets have no more corner on truth than anyone else. They could possibly draw us into the temples of a thousand false gods. Therefore, when we read a poem, we should do so realizing that ultimately we need to understand the world view embodied in the poem as much as the world view embodied in the work of nonfiction. But this is no problem. Many poems are rich in idea as well as in emotion, and their world views can be readily detected. (See pp. 51-53 for a discussion of the relevant questions.) When the world views have been de-

tected, they are subject to the same critique as world views found in nonfiction. The fact that they are expressed in poetic form qualifies the kind of critique they should receive, but does not excuse them from the bar of truth.

Dante's *The Divine Comedy*, for example, contains many poetic presentations of scholastic philosophy. These have a dramatic role within the framework of the whole poem. Moreover, the whole poem functions as a presentation of a peculiarly medieval, Christian world view. And that world view is, most people today would say, inadequate for many reasons. But, after all has been done to show its inadequacy, one very important value remains: *The Divine Comedy* recreates in the sensitive reader the shape and feel of the medieval world as one very perceptive person saw it. For centuries what Dante depicted was largely taken to be literal truth. Now for most of us it is at best a metaphor. But it is a metaphor which can help us understand the humanness of another age.

Good poetry is a window on other worlds. Some of these worlds will be like our own, but richer, more detailed, more precisely grasped. Others will be very foreign: try reading the *Bhagavad-Gita* or even *King Lear*. But well-wrought poems and works of imaginative literature can do for us what stone-cold prose can never do. They can help us grasp the full dimensions of ways of life other than our own.

There is an aesthetic dimension to poetry which keeps us from actually worshiping at the temple of Baal even if the poetry we read seems to take us into the sanctuary. When a villain on stage plunges a dagger into the heroine's tender body, we do not leap from our theater seats and seize the culprit. We know it is just a show—an imitation. As we will see in the following chapter, we experience in poetry a Secondary World—one something like the one we live in, but a creation of the artist, not of God.

Therefore, when we read the poems of despairing naturalists, we are not bowing the knee to the void. And when we grasp vicariously the sweetness of human love seen as the only tent pitched against the winds of chaos, we are not saying in our heart of hearts that there is nothing greater than human love. Matthew Arnold's justly famous poem, "Dover Beach," can be as meaningful to a Christian as to a person who has lost his faith, as the speaker in the poem seems to have done.

> The sea is calm to-night.
> The tide is full, the moon lies fair
> Upon the straits;—on the French coast the light
> Gleams and is gone; the cliffs of England stand,
> Glimmering and vast, out in the tranquil bay.
> Come to the window, sweet is the night-air!
> Only, from the long line of spray
> Where the sea meets the moon-blanch'd land,
> Listen! you hear the grating roar
> Of pebbles which the waves draw back, and fling,
> At their return, up the high strand,
> Begin, and cease, and then again begin,
> With tremulous cadence slow, and bring
> The eternal note of sadness in.
>
> Sophocles long ago
> Heard it on the Aegaean, and it brought
> Into his mind the turbid ebb and flow
> Of human misery; we
> Find also in the sound a thought,
> Hearing it by this distant northern sea.
>
> The Sea of Faith
> Was once, too, at the full, and round earth's shore
> Lay like the folds of a bright girdle furl'd.
> But now I only hear

> Its melancholy, long, withdrawing roar,
> Retreating, to the breath
> Of the night-wind, down the vast edges drear
> And naked shingles of the world.
>
> Ah, love, let us be true
> To one another! for the world, which seems
> To lie before us like a land of dreams,
> So various, so beautiful, so new,
> Hath really neither joy, nor love, nor light,
> Nor certitude, nor peace, nor help for pain;
> And we are here as on a darkling plain
> Swept with confused alarms of struggle and flight,
> Where ignorant armies clash by night.

A Christian may, however, see this poem not only as a moment in the life of one person a century ago but as a poignant cry for love and for some hint of cosmic meaning as the Christian faith ebbs away from the Western world.

All of us on our way to maturity must learn on our own. The peasant's daughter and the prince each have a common human nature. But each also has blank tablets on which experience of all kinds can write its messages. Different cultures, different ages, different environments, different parents write different messages. So born alike, people become different. And that is what makes the truly cosmopolitan education so fascinating and so endless. No human being will ever understand even from the outside all the permutations of human nature. Even less can anyone understand them from the inside. But literature—poetry, works of the imagination, even little works of the imagination—can take us inside many times and places.

To this extent poetry is a way of knowledge. It cannot be trusted always to bring us close to truth itself, but it can be trusted to show us the way the world is seen and felt by people created in God's image; fallen, yes; in error about the way things really are, yes; but human still and deserving of our understanding, our sympathy and our compassion.

To arrest, for the space of a breath,
the hands busy about the work of the
earth, and compel men entranced by the
sight of distant goals to glance for a
moment at the surrounding vision of form
and color, of sunshine and shadows;
to make them pause for a look, for a sigh,
for a smile—such is the aim [of the
novelist], difficult and evanescent, and
reserved only for a few to achieve. But
sometimes, by the deserving and the
fortunate, even that task is accomplished.
And when it is accomplished—behold!—all
the truth of life is there: a moment
of vision, a sigh, a smile—and the return to
an eternal rest.
Joseph Conrad, Preface to The Nigger of
the Narcissus

Chapter 4
The Fierce Pull
of Blood:
Reading Fiction

Like most children, I suppose, I first met poetry in Mother Goose and fiction in fairy stories. Each month as *Jack and Jill* arrived at our home in the country, my sister and I would nag mother till she read us all the stories. It was there I met Baba Yaga, a good Russian witch who lived in a house that was supported by chicken legs. We also had a few children's books. *Peter Rabbit* I loved and *Chicken Little* too. Now that I have both outgrown and grown back into these sorts of yarns, I have come to suspect that Chicken Little may have been right after all, as one graffito I have seen suggests.

These stories of imagination and magic were only the beginning. As soon as I could read well enough, I devoured *The Saturday Evening Post*. There I met Tugboat Annie and

the Earthworm Tractor salesman whose stories appeared
frequently. And there too I met A. A. Milne whose serial-
ized mystery novel, *The Red House*, kept my heart pounding
and my imagination running late into the night. By the time
we moved twenty miles into town, I had read a number of
novels, including Jules Verne's *Twenty Thousand Leagues
under the Sea*. I read that one again just after we moved and I
entered the seventh grade. Near the end of eighth grade I
immersed myself in James Fenimore Cooper's *The Last of
the Mohicans* as I spent a couple of weeks alone with my
grandfather back in the country again.

Subcreators of Secondary Worlds

I don't recount this autobiography to lament the passing
of youngsters' reading since the advent of television. Three
of my four children—all TV babies—are avid readers. That
would have been a good percentage thirty years ago. My
purpose is rather to evoke in you a positive memory (When
did you first meet fiction? Did you like it? Why?) and to suggest that we should never lose that naiveté with which we
first listened to those childhood stories of simple virtue.

As a child "listener" and later as a reader, I never asked,
Is the story true? Do rabbits really talk? Do dark red houses
appear and disappear in various parts of the forest? No,
for the time of the story all of us as children entered its
world, and we stayed there until the last sentence became an
echo. The story had made for us a separate reality, and we
really "believed" in it right up to the final line. Yet, never
beyond. When the story was over, we asked mom for
cookies, and she reminded us of the chores.

J. R. R. Tolkien describes this well:
What really happens is that the story-maker proves a
successful "sub-creator." He makes a Secondary World
which your mind can enter. Inside it, what he relates is

"true": it accords with the laws of that world. You therefore believe it, while you are, as it were, inside. The moment disbelief arises, the spell is broken; the magic, or rather art, has failed. You are then out in the Primary World again, looking at the little abortive Secondary World from the outside.[1]

This, then, is the first and most basic principle to recognize as we become conscious of reading literature well: the novelist (or short-story writer or poet) creates a Secondary World which may be "like" the Primary World (the world of ordinary waking reality) but which first has its own literary or aesthetic reality. As readers it is our task as well as our delight to enter that world with open eyes, accept it on its own merit, learn its rules and see it function.

Listen, for example, to the opening paragraph of Tolkien's story "Leaf by Niggle":

There was once a little man called Niggle, who had a long journey to make. He did not want to go, indeed the whole idea was distasteful to him; but he could not get out of it. He knew he would have to start sometime, but he did not hurry with his preparations.[2]

From the first paragraph we begin to sense the kind of Secondary World Tolkien is creating. "There was once" sounds like "once upon a time." "A little man" is the sort of descriptive phrase that does not occur in realistic description but in fairy stories. And Niggle is surely no proper name from any country familiar to us. Yet the man himself is familiar; his humanity begins to unfold and we come to believe in him.

This initial feeling is confirmed as the story develops and the Secondary World becomes more and more elaborate. It turns out to be a place where great and mysterious personal beings are working behind the scenes, indeed a fairy-story world.

The narrative, regardless of what it may suggest about life as it is outside the story, must first function on the story level, the level of the Secondary World. As readers we must first give ourselves up to the story so that we can learn that Secondary World.

Like poetry, fiction uses language in a literary way. Each sentence may look like an ordinary proposition, but the reference for that proposition has only a literary reality. This is usually easy enough to see. No one will accuse Tolkien of claiming that in the Primary World "there was once a little man called Niggle." Sometimes, however, stories contain sentences, propositions, which appear to refer to something in the Primary World. Niggle, Tolkien says, had a kind heart: "it made him uncomfortable more often than it made him do anything." This apparent appeal to the reader's knowledge of human character, however, is first a way of telling us about the person in the Secondary World.

Then, too, when the narrator or one of the characters in the story says something profoundly true (or patently false), our first response should not be to pounce on this phrase, as if it occurred in an essay, and applaud or condemn the author. That proposition is first a part of a larger whole and may not be the view of the author, but only that of his narrator or one of his fictional characters. When Mr. Sammler in Saul Bellow's *Mr. Sammler's Planet* says, "But inability to explain [God's existence] is no ground for disbelief,"[3] we know only that (true or false in the Primary World) Mr. Sammler at this moment in his growth as a person in this Secondary World states this to be so. What Saul Bellow thinks or what the novel conveys may be something quite different, even contrary.

Attention!
Aldous Huxley opens his novel *Island* with the main char-

acter, Will Farnaby, lying dazed in the mud and hearing a parrotlike bird bringing him to consciousness: " 'Attention,' a voice began to call, and it was as though an oboe had suddenly become articulate. 'Attention,' it repeated in the same high, nasal monotone. 'Attention.' "[4] A bit later, as Farnaby is finally fully awake, the bird's song changes: " 'Here and now, boys,' chanted the bird. 'Here and now, boys.' "[5] Farnaby's feathered philosopher has given an excellent expression of the next principle we need to practice when we read fiction: we must pay attention to what the writer is saying by concentrating on the here and now of our reading. There will be time enough to reflect on what we see and feel as we read. Our primary duty is to pay attention and become aware of what is really there.

We have long since, I trust, abandoned the notion that reading fast is reading better and reading even faster is reading best. If some who are reading this are students, you know you may not be able to take this slow, easygoing approach to all of your reading. But, then, know this too: in your necessary academic haste to read much you are missing even more. No wonder books we read for classes are neither as enjoyable nor as meaningful as books, even more difficult books, we read at leisure.

The Secondary World by Bits and Pieces

What is there, then, to pay attention to? What do we find when we read? In fiction we find a dazzling array of things, and we never know until we read what unique combinations we will find. In general terms, however, the world of fiction is composed of plot, character and theme, and these come via the writer's point-of-view and tone, his use of graphic description, symbol and allusion, and his narrative style, syntax and diction. In some stories we will be struck most by the plot; in others we will come away remembering the characters and almost forgetting what happened to them. In others still, our interest will be drawn to the profound insights into human nature and we will remember the theme of the story—its striking presentation of an almost eternal truth.

As we read a novel or short story, the Secondary World comes to us in bits and pieces. Sentence two piles on sentence one; paragraph two on paragraph one; characters are gradually introduced; they begin to talk; the setting becomes obvious; the atmosphere builds; the plot begins to unfold as conflicts appear and become tied to people and events. Slowly, like a big, saggy balloon, the Secondary World fills to its full shape and form.

Let us look at the sorts of bits and pieces we find in these slowly expanding worlds of fiction. Knowing how these bits and pieces tend to function will focus our awareness and make us better observers.

In the sections to follow I have drawn several examples of plot, character, theme and symbol from both fiction and drama. Dramas contain many of the same aspects of fiction, and so when we "read" a drama we are, for all practical purposes, reading fiction. We are not, of course, experiencing the drama as drama, for that requires the whole dramatic machinery—stage, actors and so forth. But to the extent that we experience plays in the quiet of our study, we can employ the same reading techniques as in fiction.

Plot. Novels and short stories tell stories, and *plot* comes as close to being *story* as any of the bits and pieces we will consider. In other words, of all the bits and pieces *plot* is the biggest and perhaps the most important.

Simply defined *plot* is the "structure of the incidents," as Aristotle first described it. He added that plot is "the imitation of the action" and proclaimed it "the soul of a tragedy."[6] He was, of course, writing about the ancient Greek drama of Sophocles and Aeschylus, but what he said some twenty-three centuries ago applies amazingly well to today's narrative art.

The "structure of the incidents," that is, the order in which the events in a story are arranged, is its plot. And that plot qualifies and brings perspective to all else.

For example, the myth of Oedipus is told in chronological order. A certain child is born; his parents hear a prophecy and try to prevent it; the boy grows up, unwittingly fulfills the prophecy and eventually punishes himself for doing so. Sophocles' play *Oedipus Rex*, however, begins after all the action except Oedipus's self-imposed punishment has taken place. The plot of the play follows Oedipus's gradual recognition of who he is and what he has done. The act of punishment (his blinding himself) even takes place off stage. The lowly messenger who brings the news of this on stage has a superb part in the play. But in the myth the messenger does not even appear. The "soul" of *Oedipus Rex*, therefore, is not the same as the "soul" of the myth of Oedipus. The "soul" of the play is the theme of self-knowledge.

So, then, we must distinguish in our reading between (1) the plot as the principle of the structure of the events and (2) the chronological sequence of events assumed or presented in the Secondary World of the novel.

The term *flashback* is probably a familiar one. We see the technique on TV all the time: one character in the story says, "Oh, I recall when grandmother visited us . . . ," the screen goes all wavy, the original cast disappears and grandmother comes into sharp focus acting grandmotherly. So the plot may well not be chronological at all. Even if it is, the ultimate reason for its chronological nature may be something rather unrelated to clock-ticking time as such.

Perhaps it will be structured along the principle of a revelation of some cosmic "truth." In Friedrich Dürrenmatt's "The Tunnel," for example, the events are narrated in chronological order, but the principle of selection of events is related to the main character's sudden acceptance of a nihilistic view of reality.

Every story has a flow of development. In the early stages, characters are introduced, the action begun, the setting is unfolded; usually some conflict or problem is introduced early on, and this is developed to some complexity. Finally, a peak or turning point is reached, the action falls away and the story comes rapidly to an end. Discerning the conflict, the characters or ideas involved, seeing its complications, detecting the turning point are all aspects of observing plot.

In understanding the plot of a story, therefore, we not only ask ourselves, What is the structure of the events? but Why these events and not others that might have been chosen during the same time sequence? What do the particular events of the story contribute to the overall shape of the Secondary World?

To understand plot, therefore, we should ask ourselves in turn these questions:

1. What happens in the story? The answer to this question functions like a paraphrase of a poem; it helps us see the skeletal action of the whole work.

2. How are the incidents ordered? That is, what is their principle of structure? The answer to these questions is parallel to the rational structure of a poem.

3. What principle of selectivity and organization governs the sequence?

4. As far as you can tell, what is the function of the sequence of events in relation to the whole work? Some possible answers are: (1) to be of interest in and of itself, like

many of the stories we read as children and even now read in detective mysteries; (2) to unmask character which in some fiction is of more interest than action; (3) to point up the moral consequences of an action or an attitude; or (4) to convey some idea or encourage some approach to life.

In answering these questions we actually begin talking about both character and theme. (In fact, I think that Aristotle's concept of plot is very close to what most critics today call theme.) It is therefore time to turn to these other literary elements.

Character. Stories happen to people; the people to whom they happen are called the characters of the story. But *character,* as we will use the term here, has a more abstract meaning. To return to Aristotle: character is "that in virtue of which we ascribe quality to the agent [performing the actions]."[7] That is, by *character* we mean the personality of a person in the story.

Who is Holden Caulfield in J. D. Salinger's *Catcher in the Rye* or Mr. Sammler in *Mr. Sammler's Planet?* We begin to understand them as we understand people in the Primary World—by how they *act* (that is Aristotle's major point), how they dress, how they speak (their language, diction, dialect, sentence structure), how they feel, how they think, what they desire, what they choose and so forth. Sometimes we learn about these aspects through a direct statement by the author. Sometimes we infer the details through dialog, imagery, symbol or the narrator's tone as he presents the actors in his fictional world. Then, too, the author may rely on allusions to some theory of psychology and deliberately present his characters in relation to, say, Freud's concept of the Oedipus complex.

How much do we learn about Holden Caulfield, the narrator and chief character of J. D. Salinger's *The Catcher in the Rye,* in the opening few lines?

If you really want to hear about it, the first thing you'll
probably want to know is where I was born, and what my
lousy childhood was like, and how my parents were occu-
pied and all before they had me, and all that David
Copperfield kind of crap, but I don't feel like going into
it, if you want to know the truth. In the first place, that
stuff bores me, and in the second place, my parents
would have about two hemorrhages apiece if I told anything personal about them.[8]

Immediately, we recognize the voice of a young boy (a few
pages later he tells us he is seventeen), a violator of polite
social convention (note the slang phrases and diction, for
example, *crap*), a dropper of names (the allusion to David
Copperfield) who in his denial actually asks us to compare
him to a great character from the literary past.

Saul Bellow's *Mr. Sammler's Planet* also begins with an
introduction to its chief character:

Shortly before dawn, or what would have been dawn in
a normal sky, Mr. Artur Sammler with his bushy eye took
in the books and papers of his West Side bedroom and
suspected strongly that they were the wrong books, the
wrong papers. In a way it did not matter much to a man
of seventy-plus, and at leisure. You had to be a crank to
insist on being right.[9]

Note what Bellow has done. He has named his main character, told his age, mentioned his bushy eye (later we learn
why it is not bushy eye*s*), given us a glimpse of his bedroom
with its books and papers and introduced us to one of the
thematic topics that will be richly developed in the next few
hundred pages, to wit, Sammler's puzzlement over the
meaning of life. The next few lines develop this theme:

You had to be a crank to insist on being right. Being right
was largely a matter of explanations. Intellectual man
had become an explaining creature. Fathers to children,

wives to husbands, lecturers to listeners, experts to lay-
men, colleagues to colleagues, doctors to patients, man
to his own soul, explained.

As the story moves on, we begin to see that, even when the
narrator is speaking as a third person, he is deeply involved
in the mind of Sammler. In fact, the story comes to us as if
we were constantly participating in Sammler's own conscious life. These thoughts on "being right" are not just the
narrator's, they are Sammler's too. And Sammler is nothing
if not a thinker. Thus one of the major conflicts the story
develops is within Sammler himself: Sammler has a mind
that demands thoughtful answers to tough questions, but
he regards that mind as incapable of really handling these
questions properly. As the narrator says, echoing Sammler,
"The soul wanted what it wanted. It had its own natural
knowledge. It sat unhappily on superstructures of explanation, poor bird, not knowing which way to fly."[10]

Aristotle's main point about character, however, has to
do with the actions a person performs. What you do proclaims most loudly who you are. So plot relates very closely
to character. What actions do the characters initiate? Do
they act or are they acted upon? What is their place in the
unfolding story? It is an important observation, for example, that, while Mr. Sammler's place in the action is central, he only initiates one action during the whole sequence
of events. This action is made at the climax or turning
point of the novel and, in addition to calling attention to
itself by its uniqueness, it tells us that something significant
has happened to Mr. Sammler.

Character alone is static, unrelated to destiny; it gives no
indication of the success or failure of the qualities that make
up the character. That is, it gives no hint of worth—moral
worth or practical worth. Action thus qualifies the overall
impact any given character has on theme.

To take an example from drama, consider Jaques in Shakespeare's *As You Like It*. Jaques is the down-at-the-mouth malcontent who throughout the play casts gloom on all joy. He is the one who gives Shakespeare's famous Seven Stages of Man set piece. "All the world's a stage," he begins. "And all the men and women merely players." Each person plays seven parts from "the infant,/Mewling and puking in the nurse's arms" through "the lover,/Sighing like a furnace, with a woeful ballad/Made to his mistress' eyebrow" and finally to "second childishness and mere oblivion,/Sans teeth, sans eyes, sans taste, sans everything."[11] It is a powerful speech—and black with despair.

Some have said that this is what Shakespeare believed about human life and destiny. But this is a grave mistake. This doleful speech is set in the brightest comedy Shakespeare ever wrote. Even the immediate setting for the speech should have given away its overstatement. The young hero, Orlando, himself not above writing sonnets to Rosalind's eyebrow, enters lovingly carrying an old man whom he has found in the woods. Here is depth of character and a sense of value not even hinted at in Jaques's speech.

But the crowning reason for seeing this speech as a dark counterpoint to otherwise excessive light is that every major character in the play gets a partner for marriage, every one, that is, but Jaques. And though Jaques is invited to live at court with the community of married couples, he chooses to remain in the forest at the Duke's "abandoned cave."

Shakespeare has thus created a Secondary World with a spokesman for despair, but he has given all the life and power to his spokesmen for hope. The course of the action shows us this.

Take another example, this time from "Cinderella." What happens to the wicked stepmother and stepsisters?

Who gets the prince? What then is this story's commentary on the pains and rewards of simple virtue? What kind of Secondary World has the storyteller created?

In understanding character in any given story we may find the following sequence of questions helpful:

1. Who are the major characters in the story? What minor characters play at least a supportive role?

2. What kind of person is each major character? (List traits; reflect on how you came to discern these traits.)

3. What happens to each major character? How is each involved in the plot and with the others? What does their ultimate fate in the story indicate about their relation to the theme or themes involved?

4. What role does each of the characters play in the unfolding of the various themes in the work?

5. Does the author seem more interested in plot, in character or in theme? How do you know?

Again we notice in this sequence of questions, like those on plot, how easy it is to begin to talk about character and then slip into talk about plot and then, very soon, into talk about theme—the dimension of ideas. Eventually, we get around to what a work of fiction means. But as soon as we do, we should remember that fiction is like poetry: *what* a novel means is never far from *how* it means. And that throws us back on our analysis of bits and pieces.

Theme. The third major aspect of fiction is theme, the dimension of ideas—ideas about human nature and the nature of reality (metaphysics), ideas about how we know (epistemology), ideas about good and evil (ethics), even ideas about God (theology). Sometimes the word *theme(s)* is used to mean the topic(s) or subject(s) that are present in a literary work. For example, some of the themes in *Hamlet* are guilt, justice and indecision. But we will use the word *theme* in this section to mean something more specific. The theme of a literary work will be taken to mean "the insight or cluster of related insights the work expresses" concerning some aspect of human experience.[12]

Aesop's fables are excellent examples of how theme relates to story at its most primitive level. Take, for example, "The Dog and the Shadow":

> It happened that a Dog had got a piece of meat and was carrying it home in his mouth to eat in peace. Now on his way home he had to cross a plank lying across a running brook. As he crossed, he looked down and saw his own shadow reflected in the water beneath. Thinking it was another dog with another piece of meat, he made up his mind to have that also. So he made a snap at the shadow in the water, but as he opened his mouth the piece of meat fell out, dropped into the water and was never seen more.
>
> "Beware lest you lose the substance by grasping at the shadow."

Here the theme, or moral, of the story is tacked on at the end. We can't miss it. In a fable all of the details are there to contribute to the message. The story might have contained all sorts of events and actions—How did the dog come by his first piece of meat? How hungry was he? In what country does he live? The possibilities for development are endless. But only the bare bones of narrative are present, presumably because the storyteller is interested more in cleverly illustrating or capturing an idea than in constructing a plot or developing the character of the dog.

Closely related to fables are parables. Both are short narratives that illustrate a moral truth, the word *fable* usually being reserved for animal stories. Jesus' parables of The Sower and the Seed (Mt. 13:1-23; Mk. 4:1-20; Lk. 8:4-15), The Prodigal Son (Lk. 15:11-32) and The Good Samaritan (Lk. 10:25-37) are perhaps the most well known of all.

In the parable of The Good Samaritan Jesus tells a story
in answer to a question put to him by a lawyer. The lawyer
is trying to avoid the implications of the Old Testament
teaching that one must love his neighbor as himself. So the
lawyer asks, "Who is my neighbor?" Jesus' reply is interesting because it not only points up a teaching about living
righteously, but illustrates a reader's need to read well.
Even simple stories can be misread. Here is the whole context and the parable:

> And behold, a lawyer stood up to put him to the test, say-
> ing, "Teacher, what shall I do to inherit eternal life?"
> He said to him, "What is written in the law? How do you
> read?" And he answered, "You shall love the Lord your
> God with all your heart, and with all your soul, and with
> all your strength, and with all your mind; and your
> neighbor as yourself." And he said to him, "You have an-
> swered right; do this, and you will live."
>
> But he, desiring to justify himself, said to Jesus, "And
> who is my neighbor?" Jesus replied, "A man was going
> down from Jerusalem to Jericho, and he fell among rob-
> bers, who stripped him and beat him, and departed, leav-
> ing him half dead. Now by chance a priest was going
> down that road; and when he saw him he passed by on
> the other side. So likewise a Levite, when he came to the
> place and saw him, passed by on the other side. But a
> Samaritan, as he journeyed, came to where he was; and
> when he saw him, he had compassion, and went to him
> and bound up his wounds, pouring on oil and wine; then
> he set him on his own beast and brought him to an inn,
> and took care of him. And the next day he took out two
> denarii and gave them to the innkeeper, saying, 'Take
> care of him; and whatever more you spend, I will repay
> you when I come back.' Which of these three, do you
> think, proved neighbor to the man who fell among the

robbers?" He said, "The one who showed mercy on him."
And Jesus said to him, "Go and do likewise." (Lk. 10:25-
37)

Question: Does Jesus answer the lawyer's question, "Who is
my neighbor?" Re-read the parable carefully. Most readers,
I think, assume that the neighbor is the man who was
robbed; since he is "my neighbor," I must help him. But
that is not the way Jesus is using the concept of neighbor.
Rather, he asks the lawyer which one proved to be a neighbor to the man who was robbed. The lawyer names the
Samaritan, as is proper. And then Jesus says, "Go and do
likewise." That is, he says, *Be a neighbor.*

In effect, Jesus is refusing to answer the question posed
in the lawyer's terms. He is not about to quibble over who
someone has to be in relation to you before he is your neighbor and you have to love him "as yourself." Rather, he calls
the lawyer himself to be a neighbor, to act out the characteristics of neighborliness and thus fulfill the demands of
the second commandment of the law.

The Good Samaritan parable also illustrates the thematic
use of character. The Samaritan, of course, is the good
neighbor; he performs the acts of mercy. The priest and the
Levite are religious persons whose religiosity has no moral
substance. Jesus chooses the outcast Samaritan (with whom
the "Jews have no dealings" [Jn. 4:9]) to represent righteous
people, and he chooses the religious leaders of his and the
lawyer's own people to represent unrighteous people.
Again, as with Aesop, there is no character development.
Jesus gives only enough detail to show us that the Samaritan
was indeed a very generous, gracious, unbigoted person.
We know nothing else about him, nor do we need to. The
character is there not so that we can understand him but so
that we can see the moral to which the story points: we
should all be good neighbors.

When the thematic use of character becomes complex, we call the result *allegory*. An allegory is "an extended narrative which carries a second meaning along with its surface story. Generally, the characters in an allegory do not have individual psychologies but are incarnations of abstract ideas."[13] John Bunyan's *The Pilgrim's Progress* is perhaps the best-known allegory. The characters bear their essence in their names: Christian, Obstinate, Pliable, Master Worldly Wiseman, Giant Despair, for example. And the journey takes Christian from the City of Destruction through such places as the Slough of Despond, Doubting Castle, the Valley of Humiliation, the Valley of the Shadow of Death, the Delectable Mountains, the Enchanted Ground and on to the Celestial City.

Despite the simple sounding names and ideas, *The Pilgrim's Progress* is a complex work rich in theological and psychological insight. The theme concerns the pilgrimage all Christians make as they become believers and seek to live out their lives in a world that is uncongenial to Christian faith. At one time *The Pilgrim's Progress* was the book most read by Christians with the sole exception of the Bible. It would be better for Christians if that were true today.

Most fiction is not essentially allegorical. The relation between theme and plot or theme and character is usually not so direct. In *The Plague*, for example, Albert Camus to some extent uses characters thematically, but the major characters are far more than incarnations of a single concept. Jean Tarrou and Dr. Rieux embody the ideals of atheistic existentialism, but both are unique in personality and act out their existentialism in their own ways. Moreover, the existential ideas they hold and represent are given long and elaborate development in the course of dialog, reflection and action. Father Paneloux likewise represents a stance toward life—a form of Christian existentialism—but he is a full-blown person who is not to be reduced to an idea.

Some of the minor characters are more allegorical. The old Spaniard is a sheer nihilist. Cottard represents an explanation and illustration of the possibility of evil in a world where there is no transcendent standard for the good. Michel exemplifies the person who refuses to live "authentically," that is, refuses to accept the basic absurdity of existence. (Tarrou and Rieux contrast with Michel at this point.) But these and a number of other characters are woven into an ornate fabric whose total theme is complex and profound.

When a story does become complex, then, and moves from allegory to a greater realism, how does a reader come to know just what the theme is? Often the determination of theme in terms of a precise proposition (like those at the end of Aesop's fables) is not easy. Some works are so complex as to yield only to more attention than most readers are willing to give. I have never read James Joyce's *Ulysses* partly for that reason. And, while I might give it a go before I die, I doubt that I will even crack the spine of *Finnegan's Wake*. Perhaps if I come to enjoy Joyce as much as I do Saul Bellow, I will change my mind.

Saul Bellow's *Mr. Sammler's Planet* is a novel whose theme (or co-themes, really) are difficult to formulate precisely, but certainly it is not hard to know the topics treated or list the ideas dealt with. We have already seen how the novel opens (see pp. 100-01). The first paragraph introduces us not only to a character but to a series of ideas: the problem of human understanding itself, the desire to know, the failure to know. Within the first five pages Bellow has revealed much about Sammler's nature and personality. Then at the end of the tenth paragraph, after telling us how

Sammler has seen the life force in older men and women refuse to give up, the narrator (Sammler's alter ego) says, "No
one made sober decent terms with death."[14] In my copy of
the novel that line bears a double underline (for me that
means *very important*). I have read this novel many times,
but I am fairly sure that that mark came from my first
reading. In any case, as one reads further and further into
the novel, the ideas of death and the problem of human
understanding arise again and again.

Here is the point: when you see an idea introduced, then
picked up later and repeated or varied perhaps a third and
fourth time, you know you have located a thematic topic.
When this is apparent, you can keep your eyes out for further allusions and developments. Begin to underline these
places; put cross references in the margins. When you have
finished reading the work for the first time, re-read it or at
least review it. You will find many more thematic hints this
time and eventually you will be able to formulate for yourself the theme of the work.

Mr. Sammler's Planet, for example, ends with Mr. Sammler mentally praying over the dead body of his friend Elya
Gruner. And what is he doing? Accepting the possibility
of human understanding and making sober, decent terms
with death! How is this possible? Well, that's in the two hundred eighty some pages that separate the introduction of
the issues from their resolution.

In understanding theme, we may find it helpful to consider the following questions:

1. What ideas are introduced, alluded to, labeled, discussed?

2. Which of these ideas is most central to the action?
How does it (they) relate to the plot? If you have analyzed
the plot already, you may be able to grasp the theme without much difficulty. As I have tried to emphasize, plot and

theme are almost the same thing, if we mean by plot the controlling, unifying concept of the action. For example, the plot of *Oedipus Rex* is the pattern of Oedipus's self-recognition and its consequences. The theme is virtually identical with this pattern or plot: when a guilty person with high moral standards suddenly perceives his own moral guilt, he is driven to self-abrogation and almost to despair; the moral order of the cosmos cannot be abrogated.

Likewise, the plot of *The Pilgrim's Progress* is closely related to its theme—an extended statement about the course of a Christian's life from conversion to glorification.

3. What part do the characters play in relation to the theme? Do any of them present or represent a key idea in the story? What happens to these characters? Do the good survive and prosper, the evil perish? Or do the characters appear to have no moral dimension at all (like Meursault in Camus's *The Stranger*)? In either case, what kind of Secondary World does the story have?

4. What vision of life does the story convey? This is really the final question in the sequence of all questions about a particular work of fiction. Here we are dealing with the world view of the literary work and, perhaps, the world view of the author as well, at least of the author at the time this particular work was written.

Here, then, is the place to ask the sort of world-view questions we asked of Pamela McCorduck's essay (see pp. 51-53): (1) What conception(s) of prime reality is (are) pictured in the novel? Which conception is the controlling one, the one the literary work seems most to adopt? (2) What is the nature of existence as pictured in the work? Is life chaotic, orderly? Who or what is in charge of the significant events in life? Nature, God, people, society? (3) What view of man emerges? What conceptions of human nature are considered? Which seems predominant? Are human beings considered significant? Why? How much knowledge can and do they have? Why? (4) What is assumed to happen to poeple at death? (5) How are moral questions treated? Is morality seen to be relative, or is it based on an absolute? (6) What is the meaning, if any, of the overall pattern of mankind's actions? Does history have a purpose?

When the world view is really out in the open, it becomes subject to the same critique as the world view of an essayist. It is no more likely to be true or false than that of a philosopher or anyone else. Art does not change reality. A powerfully persuasive novel which, like Joseph Heller's *Catch-22,* presents the universe as ultimately absurd does not make the universe absurd. Joseph Heller, who wrote this brilliant novel, is no more privy to truth than anyone else. He has, however, written a story which makes a strong literary case for nihilism.

Nonetheless, we as readers must now view that presentation with the same critical acumen with which we view discursive arguments (like McCorduck's) for new ethical values. Since the course of analysis is largely the same as that for arguments in prose, I simply refer my readers to pages 40-53 in chapter two.

Still, we must give this warning again. The Secondary World is our first concern in reading. While we are in that world—and we should be or we won't understand it—we hold in abeyance our critical questions. Only after we have vicariously experienced the here and now of this Secondary World—nihilist or not—should we begin our critique and ask if this vision of reality is true or not.

A Few More Bits and Pieces

Plot, character and theme are primary aspects of fiction, and they deserve the major part of our attention. There are in addition many other aspects which are also involved. We will take up a few of the more important ones here.

Point of view. The term *point of view* is a technical one; it is not to be equated with idea or perspective on life. Rather it means the standpoint of the narrator of the story. Who tells the story?

In *The Catcher in the Rye*, for example, the narrator is Holden Caulfield, the major character in the story. We see everything through his eyes. Of course, as readers we see more than Caulfield does, because his words and actions, like our own, reveal more than he intends. When he uses slang and vulgar language, he apparently does so to show how grown up he is. What he reveals, however, is how adolescent he is. In any case, the Secondary World of *The Catcher in the Rye* is deliberately filtered through Holden Caulfield. We are limited as readers to Caulfield's observations and perspective and what we can discern between the lines, as it were, through coming to know Caulfield's personality—his strengths, his blind spots and so forth.

There are, of course, other points of view. It would probably help to put them in outline form because, looked at in this way, they have a certain symmetry. There are two possible "persons" that can be used and divisions of each of these:

I. First person
   A. Major character
   B. Minor character
II. Third person
   A. Omniscient
      1. Editorial omniscient (the narrator passes judgment on the characters and action)
      2. Objective omniscient (the narrator only depicts; he does not pass judgment)
   B. Limited (usually to a specific character)

1. Major character
2. Minor character

We have already seen an example of the *first person, major character* form. The *first person, minor character* form is found in F. Scott Fitzgerald's *The Great Gatsby,* as Nick Carraway tells the story of Jay Gatsby and Daisy Buchanan. Here the novelist takes a stance that allows him to tell the story from a place outside the central action. Just how far outside depends on the specific relation of the narrator to the central action.

With the *third person, editorial omniscient* the narrator is equivalent to God in the Secondary World. He makes up the story and theoretically knows everything. He can move at will into or outside of the minds of the various characters. Aesop's fables employ this point of view, as does Tolkien in "Leaf by Niggle" and Graham Greene in *The Power and the Glory.* This point of view gives the novelist the most freedom in constructing his Secondary World, but it also gives him the problem of how to avoid making readers feel as if they are being manipulated. Let's say a novelist sets up a problem in the opening of the story which would be solved if just one more piece of information were given: Why withhold this until the last chapter? Only to keep the reader reading? "Foul!" cries the reader.

Writers therefore often select a point of view which will allow them to tell the story with legitimate suspense and that often involves some limits on the omniscience of the narrator. One limit is for the narrator to refuse to comment on his characters or their action. He just depicts and that's all. Two superb illustrations of this *third-person, objective omniscient* point of view are Flannery O'Connor's "A Good Man Is Hard to Find" and Ernest Hemingway's "Soldier's Home." The narrators get inside the minds of their characters but they do not judge. All judgment, if you will, comes from the plot and from the perception of readers as they see how the events are structured and apply their own sense of values to the unfolding narrative.

The final general category, *third-person, limited,* has a further limitation. Here the narrator restricts himself to the perspective of one of the characters in the story, either a major character or a minor character. This point of view comes very close to the first-person point of view in terms of what the narrator can "know," but the style of the presentation is the narrator's and not that of the character to whom he limits himself. Moreover, the narrator can know more about the inner workings of the character whose perspective he chooses than the character himself. Saul Bellow uses this point of view in *Mr. Sammler's Planet.*

There are, of course, other variations on these forms. In the *stream of consciousness* techniques (used by Joyce in *Ulysses,* for example) the author tells the story by recording the flow of conscious monolog in one or more characters. Then too, William Faulkner in *As I Lay Dying* shifts back and forth between characters; each chapter is told in the first person by "interior monolog," the whole story being constructed like a crazy quilt of different voices all pieced together into a single work. It's a difficult novel to read, but its grim vision of reality is etched into the reader's consciousness as he gradually pictures in his mind the shape and form of the novel's Secondary World.

Obviously the narrative point of view is important to the overall effect of the literary work. It is the grid through which the story is told, and thus qualifies what we conclude concerning the issues of world view. For, just because the narrator is a naturalist or a Christian or a pessimist or whatever does not mean that the overall world view of the novel is any one of those. It just means that these world views are acknowledged as possible within the Secondary

World. The reader is left to determine by other means what the philosophic perspective of the whole work is.

One of the hints as to the relation of any part to the whole is given by tone.

Tone. The tone of a novel is the attitude the author takes to his subject. The story may be told with a flat matter-of-factness. Here the reader is expected to take the narrative in a straightforward manner. Or the narrator may soon tip his hand that he is intending a heavy measure of irony. One of the characters in Kurt Vonnegut, Jr.'s *Cat's Cradle* says, at one point, "Mother cooked a big breakfast. And then, when she cleared off the table, she found a quarter and a dime and three pennies by Father's coffee cup. He'd tipped her."[15] This little detail signifies the character of the father, of course. And, if this sort of comment were isolated, we could consider its contribution to tone insubstantial. But, if it turns out, as in this novel, that this is just one item in an endless series, we must take the emerging tone of irony and sarcasm—indeed, whimsy—into account.

Humorous, witty, sage, reflective, stern, light-hearted, droll, morose, gloomy, bright: these and many other such terms are frequently appropriate in labeling the tone of a literary work. Whatever the tone, it often contributes significantly to the theme.

For example, there seems to be a tension between the tone of *Cat's Cradle* (whimsy) and the content (how the world ends). That tension is central to Vonnegut's vision of reality. For Vonnegut seems to be saying through the novel that the fate of the human race is to disappear from the universe as absurdly as it first appeared. So what significance has life, after all? Why be concerned for the value of a valueless existence? We may as well laugh our way to oblivion.

If it is important to discern the tone of the whole work, it is also important to notice variations in tone from section to section or from one character's speech to another. There may even be a pattern to the shifting tone. Stern and sage in one section, whimsical and ironic in another. Noticing these shifts will help you feel what the writer is trying to get you to feel and perceive.

Symbol. One important way that meaning comes through the details of a story is by symbol. A symbol is a person, place or thing which stands for something else unnamed. It is like one-half of a metaphor. I could say, "My love is a rose," and then go on to describe the rose (as a stand-in for my love). Metaphors are not difficult to grasp. However, if I only talked about a rose, you might not know I was really talking about something else. That makes symbols somewhat harder to recognize and harder yet to grasp fully.

Some symbols are fairly easy to recognize. References to the cross often imply the whole world of Christianity or at least set us to summon that up in the background. But often symbols are rather local in reference. In F. Scott Fitzgerald's *The Great Gatsby,* for example, a huge sign advertising the services of an oculist is referred to several times, and eventually it becomes identified by one character as the eyes of God.[16] Likewise, the novel has numerous references to clocks; here is a constant reminder in terms of a concrete detail of an issue which is central to a major theme in the novel—the notion of time.

In William Faulkner's "Barn Burning" fire is an obvious symbol of despair and rage; it is closely tied to Abner Snopes's fierce rebellion against a world order in which he does not fit. But blood is also a symbol, as we can detect by noting how many times the word occurs and the contexts in which it occurs. We find it first in the opening paragraph of the story: "the old fierce pull of blood"; then later, "the old grief of blood" and "in his [Abner's] blood an inherent voracious prodigality." Abner is said to have a shape that is "bloodless." Yet he says to Sarty, his young son, "You got to learn to stick to your own blood or you ain't going to have any blood to stick to you." Later still Sarty is running to the stable to get Abner oil for burning another barn and the narrator says, "Then he was moving, running, outside the house, toward the stable: this the old habit, the old blood which he had not been permitted to choose for himself, which had been bequeathed him willy nilly and which had run so long (and who knew where, battening on what of outrage and savagery and lust) before it came to him." Finally, there is a reference to Sarty as he ran away from home, "blood and breath roaring."[17]

These kinds of references to blood signal that something significant to the Secondary World is being revealed. In this story at least some of that significance is fairly evident. The blood seems to carry the propensity for rage. Abner and thus Abner's son, Sarty, both participate in the sins of the fathers being visited upon the third and fourth generation. The "fierce pull of blood" links the present young generation, Sarty, to the older generation, Abner, and he in turn is linked to his forebears. Who knows the origin (*where* that blood had fed, and on *what* sort of *rage and savagery*)? And who knows why (for the blood had been bequeathed *willy nilly*)? Readers of Faulkner will know the "fierce pull of blood" to be a major theme in much of Faulkner's writing and may come to see it as Faulkner's symbol for original sin. But, even apart from this larger context in Faulkner's total work, blood is clearly a symbol in "Barn Burning" and one which contributes to the overall impact of the story.

There are no perfect rules for locating symbols and determining their meaning, but keeping the following guidelines in mind should help.

1. Are there any references to public symbols such as a

church, synagogue, cross, flag? What relation do these bear to the ideas in the story? Or to certain characters in the story?

2. What details—words, objects, descriptive phrases, allusions—are repeated? How do these relate to the ideas or characters in the story? Often the storyteller will convey the personality of his characters through symbolic use of, for example, animals. In John Webster's *The Duchess of Malfi,* a grim seventeenth-century drama, the Duke is likened to a wolf and the Cardinal to a fox. Both act beastly and the language they speak is appropriate to their beastly character.

Allusion. Storytellers frequently refer to familiar events and places, to persons in other fictional works or in the Primary World, or to ideas or phrases found in classic texts such as Shakespeare, Plato, Aristotle, the Bible. Sometimes these are not flagged, and as readers we are supposed to know what the allusion means. Recall, for example, Holden Caulfield's reference to "all that David Copperfield kind of crap" in *The Catcher in the Rye* or Matthew Arnold's allusion to Sophocles in "Dover Beach."[18]

There is really nothing short of avid reading and a pretty good memory that will prepare you for these allusions. Of course, the Christian who reads the Bible regularly will be in much better shape to read English literature of the past few centuries than a person whose knowledge of the Bible is severely limited. *Paradise Lost* and *The Divine Comedy* yield their shape and meaning more readily to a narrowly read Christian than to a broadly read secular humanist. On the other hand, a reader who has absorbed Greek and Roman mythology as well as the Bible will be in even better shape.

For those who wish to follow the leads that allusions provide, I suggest a King James Version of the Bible, a small concordance such as *Cruden's Concordance to the Holy Bible,* and a guide to Greek and Roman mythology such as *Bulfinch's Mythology* or Edith Hamilton's *Mythology*. These are readily available in inexpensive paperback form. *Style.* We come now to a fairly subtle aspect of fiction. Style is notoriously difficult to describe or define. We shall take a fairly limited definition for our purposes here. By *style* I mean the peculiar characteristics of the sentence structure and the diction of a short story or novel.

Let us take up these two aspects by reference to two very different examples from two major twentieth-century writers. The first example is from Ernest Hemingway's "Soldier's Home." This is a very short story about Harold Krebs who has returned from World War 1 and finds life back in his Oklahoma home town not just dull and boring but essentially meaningless. He can muster no interest in girls, in marriage, in a potential career or even in a job. At the turning point of the story his mother, who has done all she can to make adjustment easy for her son, confronts Krebs with reality as defined by their social context: Krebs should begin to take out the local "nice girls" and get some kind of job. "You've got to make a start at something," she says. Then the following conversation ensues:

"Is that all?" Krebs said.

"Yes. Don't you love your mother, dear boy?"

"No," Krebs said.

His mother looked at him across the table. Her eyes were shiny. She started crying.

"I don't love anybody," Krebs said.

It wasn't any good. He couldn't tell her, he couldn't make her see it. It was silly to have said it. He had only hurt her. He went over and took hold of her arm. She was crying with her head in her hands.

"I didn't mean it," he said. "I was just angry at something. I didn't mean I didn't love you."

His mother went on crying. Krebs put his arm on her shoulder.

"Can't you believe me, mother?"

His mother shook her head.

"Please, please, mother. Please believe me."

"All right," his mother said chokily. She looked up at him. "I believe you, Harold."[19]

How could any passage be more clearly and sparsely written? The sentences are exceptionally short; there are few subordinate clauses. The tags on the dialog are simple ("Krebs said" or "he said") or completely missing.

The diction too is simple. A child could understand it.

Yet, upon examination, there is considerable subtlety. When Krebs admits to his mother that he doesn't love her, she takes this as a personal affront. When he adds, "I don't love anybody," she doesn't know Krebs is revealing his total alienation from all other human beings. His problem is universal ennui, not just a family falling-out. So he tries to rectify his failure to communicate by lying, and he succeeds. In fact, in the few paragraphs that follow, Krebs allows his mother to pray for him and thus violates whatever was left of his own self-respect.

We are concerned here, however, about the style itself—and its relation to other aspects of the story. What does Hemingway's style have to do with the character of the Secondary World of the story? For one thing, there is an amazing correlation between the simplicity of the style (few subordinating clauses) and the flatness of Hemingway's universe. In "Soldier's Home" there are no real values, only mores which the chief character rejects. On what basis he doesn't seem to know. There is just no appeal to any values outside or above himself.

Second, there is no meaning beyond facticity. Things are, that's all. And thus the flatness of the world in the story is mirrored by the flatness of style. No rich sentences, no exotic words. Hence, there is no sense of wonder or awe or mystery in the story. And while we as readers may be touched by the quiet despair of Krebs, we recognize that this is due more to Krebs's perception of value than to any lack of value in our own Primary World.

Our second example is the opening section from William Faulkner's short story "Barn Burning":

The store in which the Justice of the Peace's court was sitting smelled of cheese. The boy, crouched on his nail keg at the back of the crowded room, knew he smelled cheese, and more: from where he sat he could see the ranked shelves close-packed with the solid, squat, dynamic shapes of tin cans whose labels his stomach read, not from the lettering which meant nothing to his mind but from the scarlet devils and the silver curve of fish— this, the cheese which he knew he smelled and the hermetic meat which his intestines believed he smelled coming in intermittent gusts momentary and brief between the other constant one, the smell and sense just a little of fear because mostly of despair and grief, the old fierce pull of blood. He could not see the table where the Justice sat and before which his father's enemy (*our enemy* he thought in that despair; *ourn! mine and hisn both! He's my father!*) stood, but he could hear them, the two of them that is, because his father had said no word yet:

"But what proof have you, Mr. Harris?"[20]

I did not introduce this section as I did with "Soldier's Home" because as readers we are not introduced to it. Here is where the story begins. In terms of content we encounter a setting and four characters. The setting is a country store in which a Justice of the Peace is holding court. The point of view is that of an unnamed boy (later we learn his name is Sarty, short for Colonel Sartoris Snopes) whose father is on trial. A Mr. Harris is the plaintiff.

But it is the style we want to notice. And noticeable it is—the exact opposite of that in "Soldier's Home." Here are very long sentences (the second contains one hundred seventeen words) with many phrases, subordinate clauses and interruptions. On first reading, in fact, we may find the passage so rich in content and perspective as to be confusing. The first sentence is plain enough to set the stage, but the second takes us down into the inner workings of the young boy's mind and the third shows us in a long interruption his stream of consciousness. In fact, the narrator's perspective begins with the external world (the Justice, the store) and moves progressively inward to Sarty's visual sense of where he is (the tin cans of food) to his tactile sense (what his intestines sensed) to his psychological self (the sense of fear, despair, grief) to Sarty's link with the past (*the fierce pull of blood*) on into his sense of morality (*our enemy*) then back out to the external world again (the Justice's question). The turgid, grammatically loose second sentence reflects in its structure the highly complex Secondary World of the short story. Faulkner's vision of reality in this story and in all of his major works is rich and intricate. Moral ideas count; the past has meaning and so, therefore, does the present. Characters, too, are full-bodied, well developed. The mind and its running consciousness are a vital part of Faulkner's world; the unique perspective of each individual is respected and important.

The diction also plays its part in creating an atmosphere of depth. There are a host of concrete details (note the description of the canned food) in simple diction, and enough relatively sophisticated diction to call attention to itself (*hermetic, intermittent*), especially when it occurs in unique twists of phrasing (*his stomach read, the silver curve of fish, his intestines believed, the old fierce pull of blood*). We are not used to seeing language used like this and so we pause and wonder why, perhaps stand as readers in awe of the fact that in sentence structure Faulkner has come perilously close to losing his readers entirely. And yet how well he has succeeded in bringing us to feel along with Sarty the mystery of human nature!

I have chosen to examine two passages as examples of what we find as we pay attention to style. Perhaps asking ourselves the following questions will help as we read other stories:

1. What kinds of sentences and paragraphs are typical in the story? Long, short, simple, complex, reflective, factual?

2. What are the distinguishing features of the diction and phrasing? Simple vocabulary, sophisticated, professional jargon?

3. How do the sentence structure and diction relate to theme and character?

4. What kind of world, Secondary World, is revealed by the style? Moral, amoral, meaningful, meaningless, open to wonder, flat, impersonal?

5. What connection do you see between the style of the story and the vision of reality, the world view, presented in the story?

Putting It All Together

There is no point in paying close attention to detail if we fail to experience the whole work and, as it were, to perceive it at a glance—to drink it in, savor its succulent tastes and smells, feel its philosophy of life, see its vision of reality and come to grasp more fully what it means to be human.

I find great delight in close reading and great delight in seeing the panoramic spread of a novel. I enjoy both the "here and now, boys" of immersion in the Secondary World and the "there and then" of detached reflection on what is obviously someone else's view of the way things are.

As an avid reader—but one who moves slowly and often retraces his steps—I take pleasure in re-reading and re-viewing and thus re-experiencing. If you get the idea that I would like to say, "Go thou and do likewise," I only hesitate to say it because it sounds too much like sage advice, oft given, little heeded, and perhaps worthless anyway.

Still, it is important to revive the naiveté of the first reading, even the naiveté of childhood reading. We can't really do that, of course. Knowledge—the knowledge we glean as we read closely—changes that. We can't go home again. But we can go back with sharper eyes and keener awareness, re-read the novel or story, putting aside all analytic tools, and gain a view of the writer's world we would be the poorer for missing. My second long, slow drink of Robert Pirsig's *Zen and the Art of Motorcycle Maintenance* was even better than the first. I felt that I was seeing with Pirsig's eyes and feeling with Pirsig's heart. I was and still am saddened by his failure to see what I as a Christian see by God's grace. But I revel in our common humanity and our common joy in the great expanse of America's open spaces.

"Attention! Attention!"

"Here and now, boys. Here and now."

He opened the geography to study the lesson; but he could not learn the names of places in America. Still they were all different places that had different names. They were all in different countries and the countries were in continents and the continents were in the world and the world was in the universe.

He turned to the flyleaf of the geography and read what he had written there: himself, his name and where he was.

Stephen Dedalus
Class of Elements
Clongowes Wood College
Sallins
County Kildare
Ireland
Europe
The World
The Universe

. . . He read the flyleaf from the bottom to the top till he came to his own name. That was he: and he read down the page again. What was after the universe? Nothing. But was there anything round the universe to show where it stopped before the nothing place began? It could not be a wall but there could be a thin thin line there all round everything. It was very big to think about everything and everywhere. Only God could do that.

James Joyce, A Portrait of the Artist as a Young Man

Chapter 5
Cityscape:
The Larger Context

We have been plunging into the intricacies of reading. We have examined arguments and presuppositions, looked at structures and substructures of poems, and analyzed many aspects of fiction. What more can there be to being a good reader?

To answer let us return to the metaphor of the skyscraper. Poems (and the same could be said of novels, short stories and even essays) are like elaborate, well-structured buildings: they have an overall unity composed of many substructures. But skyscrapers do not exist in isolation. The Sears building in Chicago does not rise up out of nowhere and exist in relation to nothing. Much shorter buildings surround it, and buildings almost as tall peer across the cityscape slowly turning various shades of gray and brown and green. To understand the function of the Sears skyscraper, we must see not only its internal structure but its place in the city—one city, Chicago—its relation to commerce, to the arts, to the ongoing life of the city. And then we must see it as one dot in an even larger picture—the economy, the architecture, the life of the country. There is no end, this side of the stars, to the links this building has to life at large. It would be no exaggeration to say that in order to understand the Sears building fully we would have to understand the universe. And then, of course, we hasten to say, we can't do that.

Any piece of writing has equally complex links to its immediate surroundings and to ultimate reality. A poem like Shakespeare's Sonnet 73 which we so painstakingly read does not stand alone. It is first a product of an individual writer and bears his personal stamp. It is also one poem in a collection of one hundred fifty-four poems very similar in form, and that collection is one of many similar collections by other writers. Then, too, it is a poem written at one particular period of time and bears the marks of its age and national origin. It deals with a set of ideas whose links to other ideas provide an environment that goes well beyond the specific subjects dealt with in the poem itself. And finally, it comes into relation with readers by calling up in them ideas, memories, experiences and visions which are theirs alone. In short, any piece of writing exists in the larger contexts of biography, literature, cultural history, intellectual history and readers' psyches. And so to fully understand a sonnet we really need to understand everything. And, of course, we can't do that.

If this observation casts us into despair, we are in good company. Douglas Bush, for thirty years a professor of English literature at Harvard University and one of the most well-read men of our time, made this comment to a

group of his fellow scholars:
> While there may be polymaths among us who have no
> reason to be so troubled, it can probably be assumed that
> most scholars and critics have some acquaintance with
> despair, unless they early reconciled themselves to pick-
> ing up pebbles on the shore or cultivating their own small
> garden. . . . There is just too much to know, not only of
> literature itself and the vast amount of scholarship and
> criticism but of cultural history in general, since the study
> of literature takes in everything that man has felt and
> thought and done, including science and the arts.[1]

If Douglas Bush at age sixty-seven can lament his lack of
knowledge, we are all in trouble.

We will just have to realize that ignorance will always be
our lot and then get on with the task—often a joyful one—
of learning what we can with the time and abilities we have.
After all, God may be less frustrated by our ignorance than
we are. Still, he has given us minds to know and we are re-
sponsible for how we use them. There is, indeed, much that
we can accomplish.

The Biographical Context

Every piece of writing was written by a person. Some revelation! What is difficult to understand is just how much the
personal biography—the personality, character desires,
hopes and fears—of the writer is important to a reader's
understanding of what has been written.

It is important to know, of course, that Pamela McCorduck is an English teacher, respected enough to have an
essay published in a respected publication. That tells us that
she is a person whose views are likely to be broadcast widely
and perhaps acted on. This should not, however, affect our
decision regarding the ultimate validity of her proposal.
For what McCorduck says can be well understood, cri-

tiqued, and accepted or rejected without reference to who she is.

When it comes to more personal writing—such as some poetry and fiction—the author's biography may be more important. We can enjoy Hopkins's poems, like "Hurrahing in Harvest," without knowing that Hopkins was a Jesuit, a convert from Anglicanism, a man who struggled to find a legitimate place for sensuous poetry in a life that was otherwise bent toward asceticism. But the more we know about his inner life, his struggle with spiritual dryness and religious despair, the better we will appreciate the artful craft and subtle psychology of his so-called terrible sonnets written during a period of deep, inner doubt. These sonnets (called "terrible" because of their subject matter not because they lack aesthetic quality) are profound expressions of Hopkins's struggle with a God who seemed to have turned his back on him. They are not, however, an indication of Hopkins's loss of faith. This becomes clear as we read Hopkins's journals, letters and otherwise study his biography. The critics I have read who feel these sonnets do express such a loss of faith generally show by their own attitude to their subject that they do not understand the psychology of Christian faith. This sort of analysis, by the way, begins to move us close to the ideological context to be discussed below.

To document our discussion, here is one of those "terrible sonnets." In fact, it's one of the first Hopkins poems I struggled to understand many years ago:

> Not, I'll not, carrion comfort, Despair, not feast on thee;
> Not untwist—slack they may be—these last strands of man
> In me ór, most weary, cry *I can no more.* I can;
> Can something, hope, wish day come, not choose not to
>   be.

But ah, but O thou terrible, why wouldst thou rude on
  me
Thy wring-world right foot rock? lay a lionlimb against
  me? scan
With darksome devouring eyes my bruiséd bones? and
  fan,
O in turns of tempest, me heaped there; me frantic to
  avoid thee and flee?

Why? That my chaff might fly; my grain lie, sheer and
  clear.
Nay in all that toil, that coil, since (seems) I kissed the
  rod,
Hand rather, my heart lo! lapped strength, stole joy,
  would laugh, chéer.
Cheer whom though? The hero whose heaven-handling
  flung me, fóot tród
Me? or me that fought him? O which one? is it each one?
  That night, that year
Of now done darkness I wretch lay wrestling with (my
  God!) my God.[2]

After you have grasped the main ideas of the poem, ask
yourself, "Does this poem recount the loss of faith or rather
a struggle with despair with faith as the winner?" As you do
this, consider especially, *now done darkness*. And then reflect
on your own life, if you are a Christian: is this so far from
your own experience?

Note that with these questions we move away from biography into a consideration of the data of the poem itself
and on toward a reflection on our own personal experience, that is, what we will call the readers' context. In reading well we move back and forth like this all the time.

Sometimes, of course, we can know very little about the
biographical context. Shakespeare's life is shrouded in mys-

tery—much of it created by well-intentioned pseudoschol-
ars, by the way. Chaucer too we know primarily by his literary works. Yet the works of both writers stand so well
amidst their other contexts of history, literature and ideas
that we do not seem to miss much. Of course, no one wishes
we knew less.

On the other hand, sometimes we know a great deal. In
the case of Samuel Johnson some of what we know is itself
literature: James Boswell's biography of Johnson is a genuine work of art. It is perhaps fair to say that without Boswell
we would read much less of Johnson's own writing, which
tends more and more as time goes by to become "period"
literature only—something we read to get a handle on an
era rather than to enjoy in its own right. But Boswell's *The
Life of Samuel Johnson* will be a joy forever— well, almost.

The Literary Context
Every work of literature comes into being within a literary
context. The first literary context to examine is the author's
own developing body of work. Sonnet 73 was not Shakespeare's first poem. When this sonnet was published it had a
place in a collection. So to understand the sonnet well, we
should examine the whole sonnet sequence. To do so properly would be impossible here, of course.

"Barn Burning" is only one short work which Faulkner
sets in his fictional Yoknapatawpha County. The characters who appear in the story are related to other characters in other stories. So "Barn Burning" is only one small
piece in a giant jigsaw puzzle that grew larger and larger
as Faulkner brought out novel after novel and story upon
story. Actually, for Faulkner's "Barn Burning" the literary
context is far more important to the meaning of the story
than any biographical fact we can know about the author.
And with Faulkner we can know a lot.

A second literary context is the genre or type of literary work to which the specific piece belongs: essay, argument, editorial, prayer, dissertation, lyric poem, epic, novel and on and on. Shakespeare's Sonnet 73 belongs to a sonnet cycle which was one of the most popular genres of the 1590s. From 1591 to 1599 twenty-four sonnet cycles were published in England. During the next twenty years only five sonnet cycles were published; only a handful of sonnets, notably good ones from John Milton, for example, were published from 1620 to 1660. From 1660 to 1800, the genre was practically dead. Then Wordsworth and Keats began writing individual sonnets again, and since then the form has had much life. Shakespeare's sonnets were written prior to 1598 but they were not published until 1609.

These are a few of the bare literary-historical facts about the genre. To really appreciate Shakespeare's work we would need to read some of the sonnet cycles of his contemporaries, like Sir Philip Sidney, Edmund Spenser, Samuel Daniel and Michael Drayton. Then we should read a number of sonnets of succeeding eras. Because I am so attracted to the sonnet form, I have done this, and I now have, I believe, a real appreciation for what the sonnet is as a genre, what has been done with it down through the ages (Hopkins and Donne, for example, used it to great effect), and also what its limitations are. Each reader will probably want to do at least some extensive reading in one genre or one subject. Such reading has its own rewards.

In any case, we also know that in the age of Elizabeth it was considered proper for a young, aspiring poet to begin writing lyrics, sonnets and pastoral poems, then move on to larger works, such as elegies, and finally concentrate on the greatest genre of all, the epic. Shakespeare, unlike Edmund Spenser and John Milton, never went that route. But he did start down the track.

We also know that poems were dedicated to patrons who might thereby support the poet. So Shakespeare's sonnets were dedicated to "Mr. W. H.," identified as "the only begetter of these ensuing sonnets." Controversy has raged ever since as scholars have tried to identify W. H., this being considered of value to interpreting the sonnets since so many are addressed to a man. We cannot go into the issue here; the arguments are too complex and the results too uncertain to be of value for our purposes. Suffice it to say that Shakespeare's sonnet sequence sits like a skyscraper in a city in a country in a world in a universe. The city we know, the country we only guess at. We should be satisfied. After all, Douglas Bush has commented, "We can of course only achieve limited degrees of truth in trying to re-create the outward and inward conditions in which a work of art was engendered, but, unless we try, we cannot distinguish between its local and temporal and its universal and timeless elements; indeed we may not be able to understand some works at all."[3]

The more we read various kinds of literary works from various periods, the more we build for ourselves a knowledge of literary context. And, while in the short run we may use helpful guides, such as Albert C. Baugh's *A Literary History of England,* in the long run our own reading will have the most significance to us. As we read novels from Daniel Defoe to Saul Bellow, poems from John Donne to Sylvia Plath, arguments from Plato to Polanyi, our knowledge of the literary context will expand so that almost automatically we see what changes T. S. Eliot is ringing on Shakespeare, what shifts in form Henry James is making in the genre of the novel, what philosophic insight Albert Camus is adding by harking back to the themes and issues of Daniel Defoe's *A Journal of the Plague Year.* Everything we read—absolutely everything we read is related to everything else we read. One of our tasks is to see just how.

The Historical Context

Every piece of writing was written at one time (or period of time) rather than another. How obvious! And yet this simple fact is often vital to our grasp of what a writer is saying.

The realization that Shakespeare wrote almost three centuries before Freud should keep us from reading *Hamlet* as an instance of the Oedipus complex, and yet as Ernest Jones's *Hamlet and Oedipus* (1949) testifies, it hasn't done so. We are ever prone to read back into literature of a bygone era ideas and points of view that were generated decades, even centuries, later.

Knowing in depth the cultural situation of the time and place of the work we are reading will enhance our ability to comprehend it and, in turn, what we glean from reading the work itself will add to our conception of the age. To read Boswell's biography of Johnson, for example, will tell us much about Johnson's age, and knowing that will help us read not only Johnson but his contemporaries as well.

A hefty knowledge of historical data is, however, usually not required for reading a literary work; what is required is a sense of the culture, the values, the basic assumptions of the age. The latter we will discuss in the next section. But sometimes specific facts are indispensable. Jonathan Swift's *Gulliver's Travels* (1726) was not intended as a children's story but in major part as a political satire. The only way we can understand it in this fashion is to learn at least a modicum of the political history of early eighteenth-century Europe, especially England. Fortunately, there are many modern editions of *Gulliver's Travels* which contain footnotes and general introductions that open the way for our understanding. These notes are produced by people who may be mistaken, of course, and so the really careful reader will do more than glance occasionally at the bottom of the page.

Closely related to the chronological historical context is the cultural context. For example, when we read literature from a country whose heritage hardly overlaps ours at all, we will need to deliberately learn about the culture. Most Westerners will need a lot of help reading the Indian legend, *The Bhagavad-Gita*, for example. Here we not only have a story from the ancient past but from a culture whose root ideas and values must be learned from the outside in before the work can help us experience the ideas from the inside out.

The Ideological Context

As we have discussed the contexts above, we have frequently crossed over the line from biography to idea, literary context to idea, history to idea. Now we look directly at what I take to be the most important context of all—the ideological context.

All writing is born out of a stream of ideas. As we noted in chapter one, words have an "incorrigibly referential thrust."[4] They keep referring to things and, more important, to ideas. Shakespeare in Sonnet 73 talks about death and love, Faulkner about the decadence of the South and the pull of the past, Emily Dickinson about grief, Hemingway about the meaninglessness of life and so on. Ideas, ideas, ideas: they are never far from writing, not just essays and arguments but lyrics and short stories. And so it is important to see the immediate and not-so-immediate context of ideas embodied in a work.

Emily Dickinson's poem, "After Great Pain" (see pp. 59-60), is indeed composed of basic emotions and simple ideas, but the allusion to Christ in the phrase, "was it He that bore," lifts the poem out of the limited confines of one person's individual grief and places it in the universal context of God's sacrificial gift of his Son. At this point we realize how much the poet is calling on us to recognize about Christianity. She is assuming we will know about basic Christian theology: what Christ's death was supposed to have accomplished, what subsequent generations are to see in that act of "bearing" our sins and so forth. And, as readers, we must have a sensitivity to this larger context or we will not grasp the significance of the local situation. The poet's grief is not hers alone; it is the universal grief of humanity.

Matthew Arnold's "Dover Beach" (see pp. 87-88) assumes at least a basic knowledge of Western culture. First published in 1867, this poem talks about the "Sea of Faith" that used to encircle the globe. He "says" nothing else directly; the remainder is concrete detail used symbolically to summon up a feeling of the loss of faith throughout the Western world. Readers of English literature will certainly know what he refers to because the decline in Christian faith throughout culture is easy to document. In fact, Arnold's "Dover Beach" is often used as a small part of that documentation.

Sometimes, in a combination of biographical and ideological contexts, the author will comment about his intention in a work he has written or reveal something about his overall perspective on life that will suggest a fruitful way to look at his works. Albert Camus, for example, commented in 1950: "In the darkest depths of our nihilism I have sought only for the means to transcend nihilism."[5] This remark is, whether intended or not, an amazing key to his novel *The Plague*. The theme of the whole book is that in a nihilistic universe (one in which nothing intrinsically means anything, a universe in which God is dead) people can create values which are truly valuable and which, when violated, show the contrary face of evil. In short, *The Plague* is an attempt in novel form to go beyond nihilism.

Knowing Camus's own existential thought as expressed, for example, in his philosophic works *The Rebel* and *The Myth of Sisyphus* is extremely useful for grasping Camus's ideas in the novel and for experiencing the novel in the fullest way. In the straightforward exposition of his philosophic works Camus has explained his concepts of the "absurd," "rebellion" and "philosophical suicide." These ideas are incarnated in the characters and action of *The Plague*.[6]

Indeed there are today many works of existential literature—novels and plays and poems—which are deliberately written as embodiments of existential philosophy. Friedrich Dürrenmatt's "The Tunnel," for example, is a short story whose theme would be quite opaque to readers unfamiliar with the notion of the "absurd" as various existential philosophers speak of it or of "authentic" existence as understood by Sartre.

Of course, it is not just modern philosophic literature which demands from readers a knowledge of ideas. We will misunderstand much great literature of the past if we do not know how the ideological context which the writer assumed is very different from that of twentieth-century England and America.

I first read John Milton's *Paradise Lost* as a third-year graduate student in English literature. Somehow I made it through a B.A. and M.A. in English without knowing much more than Milton's name. I say this to my own shame, of course; though I am humored to think my undergraduate and first graduate schools share a bit of the blame! The point is that when I first read *Paradise Lost,* I was ready for it. I had read much literature of Milton's age and had more than a basic knowledge of the Bible, Western philosophy and theology prior to the seventeenth century. So when I leaned back—and I recall doing just that—and slowly read

Book I and then Book II, I was thrilled. Over and over, I would glance up from the page and say to a fellow graduate student in the room where we all had our desks, "Wow! This is great! Milton is a great writer!" And they would smile as if to say, "So, where have you been all your life!" To which the only good answer, I suppose, would have been, "In Nebraska shucking corn."

I went on to study Milton much more seriously. And I have been privileged to teach many sophomores a few books of *Paradise Lost* and several classes the whole of Milton's major works. But, sad to say, I have yet to find a student as enthralled with *Paradise Lost* as I was when I read it for the very first time. I felt like Keats did when he first read Chapman's translation of Homer.

> Then felt I like some watcher of the skies
> When a new planet swims into his ken;
> Or like stout Cortez when with eagle eyes
> He stared at the Pacific—and all his men
> Looked at each other in wild surmise—
> Silent upon a peak in Darien.

I believe that the difficulty of Milton—and Spenser and Dante too—is largely related to the shift in intellectual context between the twentieth and the seventeenth centuries. Literary scholar Graham Hough has said, regarding Spenser, "A gulf divides us from Spenser; but because his language is not difficult and his manner unaggressive we are not clearly aware of it. Christian, heroic, chivalrous, romantic—our world is none of these things."[7] Indeed, Hough is right: our age is secular (or, if religious, occultish and psychic), prosaic, egalitarian, cynical. Antiheroes people our novels; there are no epics. There are no ranks upon ranks of angels; our world is as flat as Hemingway's narrative style.

To read *Paradise Lost* in its proper historical context we must construct for ourselves a conception of the universe which is vastly different from that of our own century. We have to learn an old cosmology, a faculty psychology, a bit of classical logic, some Aristotelian ethics and rhetoric, a whole scheme of biblical doctrine and Reformation theology, and a good portion of Occidental mythology.

Lest this seem like an impossible task, let me hasten to add that there are a handful of easily read guides to help us. E. M. W. Tillyard's *The Elizabethan World Picture* is the place to start. His short book lays out in simple form the basic presuppositions of the sixteenth- and seventeenth-century view of the world.[8] C. S. Lewis in *The Discarded Image* covers much of the same territory in a different way and focuses somewhat more on the medieval version of this same basic view of reality.[9] His *Preface to Paradise Lost* is a superb introduction not only to the ideological context of Milton's epic but also to the literary context of the epic form.

So Milton—and Spenser, Dante or almost any other major literary figure of the past—need not remain forever foreign. There are many superb "student" editions of the classics (such as the Riverside Editions published by Houghton Mifflin, the Penguin and Pelican editions, or the Norton Critical Editions), and most of them are available as paperbacks. The best student edition of *Paradise Lost* is edited and profusely annotated by Merritt Y. Hughes and published by Odyssey. I think most Christian readers will agree that the best English annotation of *The Divine Comedy* is Dorothy Sayers's version published by Penguin.

There is no need to turn this section into an annotated bibliography. Your library or local bookstore will be glad to give you advice on editions that may help you get started in an area which you have not yet charted for yourself. Once you get the feel of an area or an author, you will need little help. In fact, you will find yourself knowledgeably disagreeing with some of the help you have received. The first useful book I read that related to the seventeenth century was Basil Willey's *The Seventeenth Century Background.*[10] When I read it, I had no way to judge its perspective. Now I find it rather wrong-headed, especially on Milton. But it is still a book I recommend to readers just getting started in the area.

Background information does not always give us the "answer" to the "meaning" of a work, but it will do something almost as important: it will keep us from making serious errors. Just how this is so we will see as we consider the context of the reader.

The Reader's Context

Every reader comes to the works he is reading with a special set of values, desires, abilities, interests, ideas. In other words, as readers we all read within the framework of our own world view. Our ability to read well depends to a large degree on just how clearly we understand ourselves and how much we realize ours is not the only way to look at reality. If—for the moments of our immersion in the writing and thus world view of another person—we are unable to detach ourselves from our own limited perspective, we will not be able to see any piece of writing on its own terms.

I am not saying that we ought not disagree with anything we read. Indeed not. We must disagree if the thrust is in opposition to what we take—after reflection, study and prayer—to be the truth. But we must also be sure that we have "heard" the other person as he or she wishes to be heard.

H. G. Rosedale, an early twentieth-century critic, once wrote that *Paradise Lost* could not possibly have been written to fulfill its stated purpose to "justify the ways of God to man" because the poem does such a bad job of it.[11] Milton, Rosedale reasons, was an intelligent person, and therefore he couldn't have taken seriously the Puritan theology he used in his poem, for Puritan theology, to this critic, was patently foolish. Therefore, Milton must have intended something else. Rosedale goes on to suggest that *Paradise Lost* is an allegory of Milton's contemporary political and religious situation. Satan represents Rome, and his entry into Paradise is a picture of the Jesuits entering England. The angel Michael is Cromwell.

This reading is absurd; I have never heard anyone other than Rosedale propose it; I have never even heard anyone comment on it. How could Rosedale have gone so wrong? Primarily, I am sure, because he had to grant that Milton was a brilliant man. A brilliant man couldn't hold what to Rosedale was not just wrong theology but stupid theology. Therefore, Milton did not believe what he wrote but used it for a cover or vehicle for something else. The problem is in Rosedale's presuppositions. Is the theology of *Paradise Lost* stupid? Few Christians in any age since Milton will answer yes, though many would disagree with many details of Milton's thought and some would say he doesn't properly "justify God's ways."

In any case, Rosedale was unable to divorce himself from his own presuppositions enough to let Milton's perspective come through clearly to him. He stands, therefore, as an example we ought not follow.

Still, all modern readers of Milton face the same difficulty as Rosedale. Not every ideological problem in *Paradise Lost* is cleared up by understanding that Milton was a basically orthodox Christian. What are we to make, for example, of the war in heaven in Book VI? Here the good angels under Michael's command fight the bad angels under Satan's command; they all wear armor and carry swords and shields. Moreover, when Michael's sword pierces Satan's side, Satan bleeds a bit of "Nectarous humor" and then the wound quickly heals:

> But the sword
> Of *Michael* from the Armory of God
> Was giv'n him temper'd so, that neither keen
> Nor solid might resist that edge: it met
> The sword of *Satan* with steep force to smite
> Descending, and in half cut sheer, not stay'd
> But with swift wheel reverse, deep ent'ring shear'd
> All his right side; then *Satan* first knew pain,
> And writh'd him to and fro convolved; so sore
> The griding sword with discontinuous wound
> Pass'd through him, but the Ethereal substance clos'd
> Not long divisible, and from the gash
> A stream of Nectarous humor issuing flow'd
> Sanguine, such as Celestial Spirits may bleed,
> And all his Armor stain'd erewhile so bright.
> (*Paradise Lost*, VI, 320-334)

Surely we cannot believe Milton thought angels wear armor, fight with swords and bleed nectar. Modern readers have a right to be baffled. If we are to understand that Milton took his theology literally, must we believe he took this "epic machinery" literally too? With a small amount of effort this question is easily answered.

Not many years before Milton wrote *Paradise Lost* he constructed for his own personal use a theology of the Christian religion, *The Christian Doctrine*. In the preface to that work he explained his reasons for belief and laid down the rules he was trying to obey as he formulated his faith. He says that he has "taken the grounds of my faith from divine revelation alone"; all of the doctrines he argues for, he claims, are "derived solely from the word of God itself."

If anyone wishes to challenge him, he is willing to rethink his position but only if the challenge is clearly based on Scripture. Like Martin Luther before the Diet of Worms, Milton accepts as authoritative no other judge or interpreter of the faith.[12]

Here, then, is the clue we need. Does the Scripture contain any reference to angels and conflict in the heavenly places? Yes, in Revelation 12:7-9, for example. Are the angels seen to wear armor, carry swords and bleed when clobbered? No. We can conclude, then, that Milton's epic battle machinery is a "fiction," a "picture," a metaphor; its reality is only in the Secondary World. The conflict between the good and evil forces—that Milton took quite seriously.

Actually, it would not be necessary for Milton to have given us this clue in *The Christian Doctrine*. We can know from a study of the theology of the age that the basic doctrines and theology in *Paradise Lost* are largely what Christians of all ages have believed. In C. S. Lewis's phrase, the theology of *Paradise Lost* is "mere Christianity." Many brilliant people of his age held this theology. Why, in the light of no contrary evidence, should we think Milton is an exception? If we know at least a little bit about the intellectual climate of the era in which the literary work in question was written, we can avoid becoming either a slave of the historical context of our own age or the victims of our own private thoughts and dreams.

It is, of course, in the reader's context that each piece of writing will ultimately be judged. Whatever an essay or poem means it means to somebody. Whatever experience "Barn Burning" creates is some person's experience. The goal of good readers is to see that *their* "meaning" is the "meaning" of the work, that *their* experience is the most appropriate to that work.

The Christian Reader

Finally there comes a time when the work has been read—the attention has been given to the pieces, to the whole and to all the contexts. The reader is satisfied, let us say, that he or she has more than the gist of the argument and has felt the work as deeply as it demands. This is the time for serious reflection that goes beyond the act of good reading to the broader acts of good living.

If we have chosen to read profound works that are well written, we will have food for thought for many years to come. We will be challenged by the fact that so many different people live such radically different lives, have such radically different ideas and desire such radically different things. In the light of such diversity we will be cast back on something to unify our own perspective on life. We will appreciate more and more the centering forces that work to keep us from rushing off in five directions at once.

Some Christians think these challenges are so great that reading any non-Christian book is too dangerous. This view is also prevalent in many modern cults. Sociologist Ronald Enroth says, "Newspapers, TV, magazines, books other than certain 'approved' religious literature—all are prohibited in most groups. As one ex-member put it, 'I had to reject my worldly knowledge—foolishness—according to their interpretation of the Bible.' "[13] Indeed, there is some reason too for this fear. Any time we are faced with a challenge to our faith, it is possible for us to change our minds.

But as Christians we know that all truth is God's truth and therefore there is nothing to fear from learning anything which is true. The major problem is error masquerading as truth. But unless we expose ourselves to other points of view and learn to analyze arguments, we may never learn to recognize error.

We have more to fear from naiveté with regard to error than we do from clear knowledge of error that we recognize as error. In seminary, for example, students study heresy as well as orthodoxy. In medical school doctors study disease even more than health. Why? So that they can combat disease as well as help keep the healthy healthy.

Still, a knowledge of the truth is the best defense against error, and that is why, just in terms of reading, our study of the Bible is so important. For it is in the Bible that we find God's perspective on life, his rules of the game, his pattern for our development. So if we read anything deeply at all, we must read the Bible deeply.

And how should we read the Bible in order to read it deeply? Amazingly, just like we read any other piece of literature. We should read its history as history, its poetry as poetry, its parables as parables, its commands as commands. All the advice and counsel given in the preceding chapters can be practiced as we read the Scripture.

There are many good books specializing in instruction on how to read the Bible. I would especially recommend R. C. Sproul's *Knowing Scripture* and Norton Sterrett's *How to Understand Your Bible*. In both of these books the basic approach to understanding the Bible is that of understanding any other piece of literature. Nonetheless, in light of our approach in this book, I would especially recommend reading the Bible world-viewishly. That is, as we discussed in chapter one, we should ask world-view questions of each biblical passage. Not all passages will answer all these questions, but it is amazing how many of them even some short passages answer. As a practical exercise in reading the Bible world-viewishly, for example, take each of the basic world-view questions discussed on pages 51-53 and examine carefully a few selected passages that are peculiarly relevant. As you work at this, you will begin to see the rudiments of the biblical world view emerge. And you will find familiarity with this world view of immense help in evaluating the world views you are encountering as you read elsewhere.[14] Here are some suggestions on where to start.

1. How does the Bible view the ultimate nature of reality? Exodus 3:13-14; Isaiah 40:21-31; 45:18-19.

2. What does the Bible consider to be the nature of the external universe? Genesis 1—2.

3. Who does the Bible say people really are? Genesis 1—3; Psalm 8; Psalm 139; Romans 1—9.

4. What happens to a person at death? John 14:1-3; Hebrews 9:27-28; Revelation 20:11-16.

5. What is the biblical basis for morality? Genesis 2:15-16; Isaiah 45:18-19.

6. How is it possible to know anything at all? Genesis 1:26-27; Isaiah 45:18-19; Psalm 19; John 1:1-4, 14, 18.

7. What is the meaning of history? Isaiah 40—48; Acts 6:8—7:60; Romans 9—11.

So Christians read the Bible like good readers read everything—with one very important exception: when we read the Bible we are reading what God wants us to know. Our criticism of other literary works rests on our unreserved adoption of the biblical point of view as our point of view. In one sense, we read the Bible critically—that is with our mind completely open to God's revelation in his Word and our critical faculties working to keep us from misunderstanding. In another sense, we read the Bible uncritically, for we hold that what it says, God says, and who are we to teach God!

It is precisely because we have such a basis as Christians that we can be so open to comprehending views foreign to our faith and foreign to the Bible. If in our reading our faith is challenged, we can have confidence that God will help us meet these challenges as we give ourselves to a study of his Word and practice what we find there for us.

One thing the Bible does not do: it does not denigrate the mind. The Bible is not anti-intellectual. Rather it gives the reasons why all of us know what we know, why we can think with some degree of accuracy and why we fail to think with complete accuracy.

The Gospel of John, for example, puts considerable emphasis on the mind and God-given human reason. In genre the Gospel of John is an argument designed deliberately to convince the reader that Jesus is the Christ (Jn. 20:30-31). In chapters 5 and 8, especially, Jesus is shown giving reasons why people should believe in him, and in the opening verses of chapter 1, the Gospel writer proclaims that the *Logos* ("meaning" itself, or "reasonableness") exists from eternity and is to be equated with God the Son.

The whole thrust of the Gospel of John would be belied if we played down the role of the mind in conversion and in grasping God's truth. We can be confident, therefore, that exposing ourselves to a vast array of ideas forcefully expressed is not tantamount to abandoning the truth. If we are committed to Christ and open ourselves daily to his teaching, we will be prepared to handle the various challenges we are sure to face. More than this, we will be able to understand the people who live around us but who do not share our faith. And thus we will be better equipped for both evangelism and discipleship.

Alice sighed wearily. "I think you might do something better with the time," she said, "than wasting it in asking riddles that have no answers."

"If you knew Time as well as I do," said the Hatter, "you wouldn't talk about wasting it. It's him."

"I don't know what you mean," said Alice.

"Of course you don't!" the Hatter said, tossing his head contemptuously. "I dare say you never even spoke to Time!"

"Perhaps not," Alice cautiously replied; "but I know I have to beat time when I learn music."

"Ah! That accounts for it," said the Hatter. "He won't stand beating. Now, if you only kept on good terms with him, he'd do almost anything you liked with the clock. For instance, suppose it were nine o'clock in the morning, just time to begin lessons: you'd only have to whisper a hint to Time, and round goes the clock in a twinkling! Half-past one, time for dinner!"

("I only wish it was," the March Hare said to itself in a whisper.)
Lewis Carroll, Alice in Wonderland

Chapter 6
A Time to Read: Knowing What to Read and When

"How do you find time to read so many books?" How many times have I been asked that question! Usually, I don't have a very good reply.

I suppose I am expected to explain how I manage my work and set aside a certain block of time sacred to the muse of reading. I certainly have no quarrel with people who plan their day down to the last minute, programming in eating, sleeping, daily devotions, working, giving alms and, of course, reading. But that is not my style, and I loathe being shackled by someone else's ironclad schedule.

The fact is I am an inveterate—nay, almost compulsive—reader. At breakfast, I read the daily paper and the cereal box. At coffee break and noon lunch, I have at hand, should conversation fail, some minor pamphlet or period-

ical. During the day my job calls for reading, not just manu-
scripts but letters and newsletters, trade journals and reports. In the evening I relax by reading again, sometimes
studying a deep theological tome that takes concentration
just to penetrate the surface, sometimes bounding gaily
through an Agatha Christie mystery. On my nightstand
right now is a collection of science fiction stories by Arthur
Clarke and (shades of college days!) a Riverside Edition of
John Bunyan's *The Pilgrim's Progress* which I am re-reading
for fun and profit. My wife reminds me that on our honey-
moon we went out on Lake of the Ozarks and she watched
me read a collection of short stories.

You see, I have a problem. I read too much. I pay attention to plot, image, character and theme when I should be
paying attention to wife, sons and daughters, the peeling
house paint and the leaking toilet tank. Actually, I need
advice about how to spend time *not* reading. So perhaps I'm
not qualified to advise others.

A Time for Reading
I can, however, say this: finding time for reading is no
different from finding time for any other so-called non-
essential good thing to do. If you can find time to do anything other than stay alive, you can find time for reading.
More appropriately: if you have found time to read this far
into this book, you can find time to read much further into
other, much better books! It's all a matter of determining
priorities, deciding what you *should* do with that twenty-
four hours God gives all of us each day.

I have no special insight on how one determines priorities for the use of time. There are some rather good books
on this subject written from a Christian standpoint and I
will just let a reference to them suffice here.[1] Of course, before you determine the specific place of reading in your

life, you should have considered your own talents, your spiritual gifts and God's general calling for you. Reading, in other words, must be considered in the total scheme of your life. Here again, I have no special insight and will once more refer you to the counsel of others. John White in *The Fight*, for example, has written a very helpful introduction to Christian living and has included a chapter on guidance.[2] And Paul E. Little's booklet *Affirming the Will of God* in its brevity and wisdom can hardly be bettered.[3]

I would like to comment, however, on the relation between reading and God's calling for you. My psychologist friends might say I am rationalizing, but I believe I have been called to be a reader. I don't have to ask God each day, "Should I read, today, Lord?" That was settled long ago as God apparently built into me a natural love for words and ideas, and then led me into a profession—first teaching English, then editing and writing—in which that love for language could find useful expression. My prayer is, "Lord, help me not to overdo it, to exceed the limits of a good thing and turn it into a curse."

So, perhaps I do have some counsel after all:

1. Find out what God is really calling you to do with your life right now. Is it to be a student, a mechanic, a typist, a sales representative, an evangelist or a combination of these and other things?

2. Consider the value of reading to the specific tasks associated with your overall calling and commitment.

3. Consider the potential value of reading to your understanding of other people, their inner longings, their ideas. If you find yourself living in a community of Mormons or deep-sea fishermen or longhair musicians, try reading a book or two that will take you vicariously into the world of Mormonism or deep-sea fishing or classical music.

4. If you find following a schedule at least half congenial, set aside some time each day or each week for reading. Don't be a slave to any schedule, of course.

5. Develop a reading plan that fits your needs, interests and abilities. See pp. 169-76 for suggestions.

6. If after doing all of this you find virtually no time for reading, then look back over the items now filling the slots on your schedule. Is reading more or less important for you than watching TV? (Note: If you didn't put that in your schedule, did you forget? Be realistic!) Is it more important than mowing the lawn? (Could someone else do that? Perhaps you don't have two teen-age sons!)

7. Re-reflect on the whole pattern of priorities of those activities that are discretionary. Can you find time for reading now? My guess is that you can and that, therefore, the only thing that will keep you from a more or less regular course of reading will be a failure to act on your own set of priorities—to place more emphasis on those activities that you yourself know are less important to you and God's plan for your life.

Personally, I find all this talk about priorities uncongenial. I am, therefore, often frustrated by what Charles Hummel calls "the tyranny of the urgent."[4] That which pulls on me at the moment gets my attention, and I tend to let the more important long-range goals take a back seat to less important immediate demands. All of us need to learn to say no—no to our family, no to our friends, no to our pastor, no to our deacons. All of our time could be spent in giving alms, so to speak. But we must also do other things. Our task before God is to learn his general will for our lives and to make decisions regarding our use of time within that framework.

In any case, reading is like any good human activity; we must find the overall place it is to play in our lives and then make specific judgments accordingly. It is indeed possible that some will read very little but the Bible and will do so to the glory of God. Still, I imagine the opposite will be more the rule: that those who read little other than the Bible do so to the detriment of themselves and to the diminishing of the radiant glory of God who is the fount of all knowledge and truth.

Reading with a Purpose

The real issue when we read is not how much time shall I spend reading but what shall I read? Every time I enter a bookstore or a library I am alternately thrilled and depressed. Look at all those good books! How can I know which ones to read?

If we have the idea that somehow, someday we will catch up on that reading we have wanted to do, we had best forget it. When we finish *the* book we've wanted to get to, we will almost certainly be prompted to read five more that have been suggested by it. We will never catch up.

But we can get on with it. My own bookshelves overflow with books I've read. Reading does get done. The point is to start and then to read well. How far we get, how many books we read, must not become the issue.

So where should we start? Let's look at it from the standpoint of purpose. Why are we reading? What do we plan to accomplish by it? Several possibilities suggest themselves. We can read for entertainment, information or perspective. We can read in order to understand ourselves, other people, other cultures, other ideas. And we may do any or all of these for personal growth or professional advancement. Of course, many of these purposes overlap. I am often entertained by a book which helps me personally and also relates to the work I do professionally. Still, it is worth looking at three of these purposes separately.

Entertainment. Reading solely for entertainment is not an unworthy use of time. If you can justify relaxing beneath a shade tree in summer or touring the Black Hills or seeing a good movie or playing a game of chess or watching television, you can justify reading for entertainment. There is something restorative in all these activities.

When you read for entertainment, your own sense of enjoyment is the key to the kind of book to choose. Here is where I advocate sheer whim. Does Agatha Christie appeal to you? Or have you found John Updike attractive before? Does a work of nonfiction draw your attention?

I always have at least a dozen unread books—I confess it's really many more than that—on hand just waiting the touch of whim. They have been purchased on one of many jaunts to bookstores. Now, for example, I have one Saul Bellow novel (the only one of his I haven't devoured), a couple of Stanislaw Lem volumes of science fiction, and various other novels and stories by Bernard Malamud, John Updike, Hermann Hesse and G. K. Chesterton. Along with these works of imaginative literature are rather too many unread volumes of theology, sociology and psychology. I have not selected them capriciously, but I may well seem, even to myself, to read them in a capricious order—unless, of course, I have some ulterior motive beyond entertainment in mind.

In any case, there they sit, a couple of rows of good books waiting their turn to be picked up, plowed through, underlined, annotated and stuffed into their proper place in my ever-expanding library. Sometimes I get a slight— oh, ever so slight—feeling of guilt that I have not read every book in sight, at least in my own den. But this passes when I remember that a book purchased several years ago has just recently been read at the rightest time possible and that I would have been unable to purchase it when I really needed it or felt the irresistible urge to read it. To me it is important to have at hand a wide variety of books to choose from. I am interested in many different areas and many different authors. My thought life takes me in five different directions at once. This may not fit your lifestyle. Fine. Do not imitate me. Rather find your own way to make reading an entertaining part of your life. Visit the library regularly or plot out a reading plan title by title for the next five years, if that (perish the thought) turns you on (perish the phrase). The point is to become natural about a potentially very enjoyable occupation.

Information. Reading for information only is, quite frankly, a prostitution of the art of reading. Nonetheless, we all find ourselves doing just that. I suggest we do it as little as possible because it is demeaning to the enterprise of fully human thought. Facts have meaning, and meaning exists only in a framework of presuppositions. Discovering the number of angels that can dance on the head of a pin entails a whole philosophy of being. Even the numbers in the telephone directory have meaning only in the larger context of Bell Telephone's system and our society's notion of meaningful communication.

Actually, we rarely get sheer information when we read. The newspaper reports on page one often show the "editorial" slant of the reporter or the editor. Some details are omitted and others given prominence while others more important to the meaning of the event may have not been noted at all. That means that when we read for information, we need to read critically, that is, we need to read for perspective.

Perspective. Most of my reading is reading for perspective. I rarely read anything, including Agatha Christie, for mere nonintellectual entertainment. That's because I enjoy paying attention to the subtleties of good writing, and when we do that we get more than entertained. We pick up a writer's conception of life, his understanding of human nature, his views of the good, the true and the beautiful; in short, we learn the author's world view and, if the work we are reading is well written, perhaps we even begin to experience that world view vicariously.

Here is where I believe reading becomes of most value. We are not just bifurcating our lives into the dull pursuit of information and world view on the one hand and the exciting pursuit of sheer entertainment on the other. We are putting together what should never be split—excitement and knowledge, joy and truth, ecstasy and value. Indeed, in such moments of reading we are living the *good life*.

But this means choosing good books—books that are well-written repositories of profound ideas. How can we be sure that the books we buy or check out of the library are really worth the effort we have encouraged in the preceding chapters? Well, we can't be absolutely sure, of course, but we can be reasonably sure.

Selecting Good Books

Even for a seasoned reader, visiting a bookstore can be frustrating. On the one hand, there are too many titles to choose from and most of them are, quite frankly, not good books. On the other hand, the bookstore often will not have the specific title you have come to buy and will have to special order it. Libraries can be even more frustrating, what with lost and stolen books and too little budget to develop and maintain a broad selection.

Still, with a little effort and some rather enjoyable reading of guides and reviews, much of this frustration can be prevented or circumvented. Selecting the books right for you begins with learning what the good books are and then making informed and intelligent decisions.

Special Lists and Collections. Fortunately, there are many guides to good reading. If your general reading goal calls for an immersion in what Matthew Arnold called "the best that has been thought and said in the world," then you could do no better than read your way into and through the Great Books of the Western World as selected by Mortimer Adler and Robert Hutchins. Many libraries have a copy of this five-foot-one-inch shelf of large tomes. If you don't like to read from a book that feels like an encyclopedia, then use the selection as a guide and secure the smaller, more easily managed paperback edition. Volume one of this set entitled *The Great Conversation* includes a panoramic view of the whole and a ten-year reading plan based on the fifty-four volumes in the set.

The Great Books of the Western World includes 443 works by 74 writers from the early Greeks up to the early twentieth century. Just recently Adler has announced a continuation of the shelf called Great Books of the 20th Century; this will include 131 works by 73 writers. The list itself has been published in *Time* magazine (March 7, 1977) and includes the work of novelists, such as William Faulkner, Saul Bellow, Franz Kafka, dramatists such as Anton Chekhov and G. B. Shaw, social scientists such as Jacques Ellul and Max Weber, philosophers such as Alfred North Whitehead and Jean Paul Sartre and scientists such as Albert Einstein and Jacques Monod.

These two guides to good reading must not be taken as *the* best of the good. But the list certainly is good and culturally important. I have, of course, not read all of the books on either list, but would rarely quarrel with the selection of any of the many I have read.

Another collection useful as a guide is The Harvard Classics. This five-foot shelf of books in fifty volumes was edited in 1910 by Charles W. Eliot, the then recently retired president of Harvard College. His collection also spans the history of the Western world from ancient Greece through nineteenth-century Europe and America. Eliot's principle of selection is instructive:

> My purpose in selecting The Harvard Classics was to provide the literary materials from which a careful and persistent reader might gain a fair view of the progress of man, observing, recording, inventing, and imagining from the earliest historical times to the close of the nineteenth century. Within the limits of fifty volumes, containing about 22,000 pages, I was to provide the means of obtaining such a knowledge of ancient and modern literature as seems essential to the twentieth century idea of a cultivated man.[5]

As can be detected from the style and approach evident even in these two sentences, Eliot's perspective is provincially Western. One must go well beyond this collection to gain an idea of "cultivated man" today. Even the idea and ideal of "cultivated man" should be challenged by today's thoughtful reader. But one could do worse than live his way through these fifty volumes as at least a running start toward a liberal education. The final volume contains a reader's guide to the whole set and a useful outline of the various kinds of writing included—history, education, science, politics, travel, criticism, biography, poetry and fiction.

A third helpful guide, prepared by The Committee on College Reading, is *Good Reading: A Guide for Serious Readers*. First produced in 1947, this annotated bibliography has been regularly revised so that its continuing editions are up to date. After its two-page sheer listing of "100 significant books," the editors (in my 1969 edition) annotate titles in twenty-six separate categories in the general areas of history, regional culture, literary types, humanities, social sciences and sciences.

Anthologies. Anthologies have long been used by literature teachers as handy minilibraries of the "best" or "most
representative" literature of an age or a type. There are too
many good anthologies to list, and so I will simply suggest
browsing through the college text sections of a local campus bookstore. My own preference in English literature is
British Literature: From Beowulf to Sheridan, edited by Hazelton Spencer, and *British Literature: From Blake to the Present
Day,* edited by Hazelton Spencer, Walter Houghton and
Herbert Barrows.[6] The selection of authors and works is
superb in my estimation, but the introductions to the various works and periods make this pair an especially excellent anthology. *Short Story Masterpieces,* edited by Robert
Penn Warren and Albert Erskine, also deserves mention.
Most of the short stories referred to in chapter four appear
there. In any case, if you want help in selecting the best of a
kind, an anthology may serve you well.

Best-seller lists. These very well-known lists are the poorest
guides to good reading. All they tell you is what is selling
best at the stores consulted. The stores are consciously
chosen to represent a fairly wide sample of book buyers, but
they still bear the marks of prejudicial selection. One bookstore manager, for example, once asked why *The Living
Bible*—one of his fastest moving books—never appeared on
the regular lists of best sellers. He was told that *The Living
Bible* wasn't really a book.

Even if the lists more accurately reflected sales, they
would still only record popularity and not quality. Nonetheless, the lists do form a sort of guide to contemporary
taste, a clue to "what's going on now" in the thought world
of the reading masses. While occasionally a truly remark-
able book climbs to the status of best seller, the list as a
whole represents the lowest common denominator of
American reading.

Among the more respectable of the general lists are those carried regularly by *Time* magazine, *The New York Times Book Review* and *Publisher's Weekly* (trade journal of the American book-publishing industry). I have found the lists somewhat less regularly published by *The Chronicle of Higher Education* an interesting indicator of college readers' tastes. Many of the books on *Time*'s best-seller list also appear (sometimes months later when they are available in a paperback edition) on the campus list. The better books, like *Zen and the Art of Motorcycle Maintenance,* tend to stay longer there than on the general lists. But junk books like Raymond A. Moody, Jr.'s *Life after Life* seem just as attractive to college readers as to the general public.

My conclusion: Use the best-seller lists only as an indication of popularity. *Caveat emptor.*

Book reviews. Book reviews are another matter. These can be extremely useful. There are three basic sources for reviews—general book-review journals, book-review sections in general interest magazines and the book-review sections in specialized magazines.

In the first category are *The New York Times Book Review* (weekly) which reviews a wide variety of books—from semitechnical books on the natural sciences and human sciences to novels, poetry and children's literature. The reviews are urbane and sophisticated; some are essays in their own right. *The Saturday Review* (biweekly) is similar in nature, but also carries many general essays, not directly related to one or more books. *The New York Review of Books* also deserves mention; its reviews are often long and highly evaluative, the perspective of the reviewer being given full scope.

A second source of general book reviews are those periodicals whose interests span a wide spectrum. *Time* magazine, *Newsweek, The Atlantic, Harper's, Commentary, The New Yorker* are examples.

Perhaps even more useful, however, are those periodicals which review books related to the journal's own field. Especially noteworthy for Christians are *Christianity Today, Eternity, The Reformed Journal, The Christian Scholar's Review* and *Christian Century.* These journals not only review "Christian" books but books Christians should read. Other specialized magazines with helpful reviews abound: *Psychology Today, The National Review* (political, conservative), *The New Republic* (political, liberal), *Scientific American, The Chronicle of Higher Education,* to name only a few.

Reviews, of course, need to be read with the same critical attention as any other work of nonfiction. Reviewers come to their task with special interests, biases and varying abilities. Moreover, the journals in which the reviews appear select their reviewers in part to square with the editorial perspective of the magazine. Even with the best of intentions, a reviewer may mislead a reader by failing to notice some characteristic of the book that is of interest to the reader but not the reviewer. If you read reviews regularly, you will come to recognize various individual reviewers and learn whom you can and cannot trust.

It will help to read a number of reviews of the same book before investing time or money in the book itself. If most reviewers find the same major flaws, you may wish to invest your time in another book. This is one reason I have not read Joseph Heller's *Something Happened;* too many reviewers found it undistinguished. So, despite my admiration for *Catch-22,* his first novel, I have not taken time to read his second.

Sometimes, however, I deliberately do not read reviews. If Bellow should publish another novel, I would clip the reviews and hold them till I have read the novel. I want to savor Bellow for myself—not through the grid of expectations set up by some reviewer whose opinion I wouldn't respect anyway if it differed from mine. Bellow is my turf. But there are only a very few authors whom I am so jealous to guard. For the most part, I use reviews to survey the books on topics of special interest to me and to help me select the ones most worth my reading.

Other helps. A few other aids to reading selection deserve mention. There are, for example, many general book clubs, such as Book of the Month Club, and even more specialty book clubs, like Psychology Today Book Club or Evangelical Books. They choose the more popular books and usually only in expensive cloth editions, but their selections do bear some investigation.

Publishers' catalogs are also useful if you know the publisher. The smaller the publisher, the more likely the specialized nature of the publications. If you find several books by the same publisher to be of special value, write for a catalog.

Finally come comments by fellow readers. These should be treated just as critically as regular reviews. If you know the source, you can judge its value. I was mildly intending to read *Zen and the Art of Motorcycle Maintenance* anyway, but when a good friend whetted my appetite I couldn't resist. And what a joy! After reading it, I gave a copy to another good friend.

Reading Periodicals

Some of the best writing and most economical presentation of important ideas occurs in periodicals. For gathering the general shape, form and current state of knowledge of a subject, there is often no better place to go. *Scientific American,* for example, is an excellent journal carrying articles by scientists but written for the generally educated reader. The articles often carry bibliographies to take the reader more deeply into the topic at hand.

But periodicals have an even more important function. If each week you regularly survey (scan wisely) a dozen or so carefully selected periodicals, and if you read selectively a modest number of articles that seem to be most relevant, you can get a fair idea of just what is thought to be going on in the world today. Notice, I say "thought to be going on," because you are only learning what writers write and editors print. Still, that is not always misleading.

One of the most valuable aspects of reading is its contribution to a person's understanding of the human condition. Periodicals can keep you abreast of the ever-present changes. What are our troubles now? What is being proposed and done to deal with them? What good things are developing? What is passing away? Where are people hurting? What can be done to help?

Politics, religion, natural science, the human sciences, education, literature, the arts—in periodicals thoughtful writers reflect on the latest developments, their meaning and significance for the future, immediate and down the road a ways.

There is no list of "best" periodicals which if we scan and read will make us walking libraries of keen insight on all matters new, public and private. Nonetheless, it is impossible to pay attention to every magazine which has a bearing on one's own interests. So I suggest spending several hours, maybe several hours on several days, surveying the periodical collection in a good library. From this you are likely to find fascinating magazines you never heard of before. You can then compile your own list of periodicals to review on a regular basis. My own list is found in the appendix.

One final comment on periodicals. As you may have noticed, if you subscribe to them, they begin to stack up, and then you can never find the one you want when you want it. I suggest clipping the relevant articles and filing them in some logical way by topic or author. I started this system a few years ago and have found it invaluable for subsequent writing and speaking. If you use a library for periodical reading, then taking notes can help—or, better yet, if your budget permits, make photocopies of the important articles and file them for future reference.

The Sea Is Awakening the Dolphins

In "The Celestial Omnibus," a beautiful and witty little allegory on the joys of reading literature, E. M. Forster captures the folly of thinking that reading has anything to do with the externals of quantity and social propriety. The hero, a young boy who epitomizes the naive childhood reader I have so often desired us older readers to emulate, wants to know what an old signpost means. It points up a blind alley, and in faded letters it reads, "To Heaven." His mother tells him it was put up as a joke, a bad joke, by a man named Shelley. This doesn't satisfy the boy, so he asks Mr. Bons. Now Mr. Bons is an authority on all such things: "He had a beautiful house and lent one books, he was a church warden, and a candidate for the County Council; he had donated to the Free Library enormously, he presided over the Literary Society, and had Members of Parliament to stop with him—in short, he was probably the wisest person alive."[7] Mr. Bons, however, agrees with the boy's mother. Shelley had indeed done it as a bad joke. But the boy doesn't know who Shelley is. So Mr. Bons asks his mother dumbfounded:

"But is there no Shelley in the house?"

"Why, yes!" exclaimed the lady, in much agitation. "Dear Mr. Bons, we aren't such Philistines as that. Two at the least. One a wedding present, and the other, smaller print, in one of the spare rooms."

"I believe we have seven Shelleys," said Mr. Bons, with

a slow smile. Then he brushed cake crumbs off his stomach, and, together with his daughter, rose to go.[8] There is a great deal going on in this passage: for example, allusions to Shelley as if he were the Bible—present in many editions but unread and unappreciated except as a symbol of social status.

The boy, however, doesn't believe the sign is a joke. He investigates for himself and learns that the sign indeed points to heaven. In fact, he buys a ticket and travels there on a coach driven by Dante. When he tries to take Mr. Bons along with him on such a trip, Bons falls out of the coach and ends in a "shockingly mutilated condition in the vicinity of the Bermondsey gas-works."[9]

Just before he falls from the omnibus, the driver urges him to approach literature with the right attitude. If Bons will do this, he too can see the charms of literature's heavenly realm (what I have called earlier the Secondary World). Dante says to him, "I am the means not the end. I am the food and not the life. Stand by yourself, as that boy has stood. I cannot save you. For poetry is spirit; and they that would worship it must worship in spirit and in truth."[10] Forster here is not, I believe, saying we should worship poetry as such. That is just his way of saying in terms of the Secondary World of "The Celestial Omnibus" that to understand and to appreciate imaginative literature (poetry and fiction) we must not first come to it for utilitarian reasons—either for social status or for a philosophy of life. Each piece of literature has its own reason for being, its own Secondary World. That comes first in order of priority as we read. Otherwise instead of greeting Achilles and Tom Jones, Othello and Iago, Frodo and Gollum, we will end in the gas-works with Mr. Bons.

If, however, we approach our reading and our reading plans in the spirit of the young boy, we may expect to be amply rewarded. The boy in the story, left alone in the coach, puts it this way: "Where have you fallen to, Mr. Bons? Here is a procession arriving to honour you with music and torches. Here come the men and women whose names you know. The mountain is awake, the river is awake, over the race-course the sea is awakening those dolphins, and it is all for you. They want you—"[11] Indeed, great books teem with peoples and lands, with ideas and attitudes, with exuberance and life. Let us take our fill, doing it slowly, thoughtfully, imaginatively, all to the glory of God.

Appendix

Appendix:
Reading with a Plan

Till now I have avoided suggesting a reading plan. To me such plans suggest programmed learning, potted thinking. To think well is to shun all such directed lines of reading and to go where truth, as you discover it, leads. Still, it is certainly useful to get an overall picture of the country one is traveling—to know where that country is in relation to the rest of the world and know the location of its natural features, the lakes and rivers, fields and forests, cliffs and caves. A liberal education is supposed to do this, of course, and reading as I have tried to encourage it is a liberal education.

Reading Books with a Plan
Getting an overall picture is what reading world-viewishly is all about. I have described this most fully in chapter two (especially pages 40-53). Here I would like to suggest a more systematic

approach to learning what the current world views are. As we become familiar with the general features we will begin to see the variations, and then, as we read more and more, we will see the permutations of these world views, see how they appear in writing as different as lyric poetry and political science.

This systematic approach is based on my own book *The Universe Next Door,* an extended discussion of the most pervasive current world views. The plan consists of reading a chapter from that book along with a series of other novels, short stories and works of nonfiction which present or illustrate these world views. The goal I have in mind for any who wish to follow this plan is to develop a consciousness of the patterns of thought actually held by people today. A conscious immersion in the various world views provide an excellent background for any further reading done on your own—by plan or by whim.

One comment on this list may be appropriate. Many of the works listed are more complex than the single category into which I have inserted them. Both John Updike's *Rabbit Run* and Saul Bellow's *Mr. Sammler's Planet* present a series of characters who themselves illustrate different world views. The plots in which these characters work out their destiny show these world views in various stances of conflict with each other. Bellow's novel, by the way, is not so much Christian theism as a variation, a sort of mystical Judeo-Christian theism.

General Introduction

James W. Sire, *The Universe Next Door*
Francis A. Schaeffer, *How Should We Then Live?*
Brian Walsh and Richard Middleton,
   The Transforming Vision

Christian Theism

Nonfiction

John R. W. Stott, *Basic Christianity*
J. I. Packer, *Knowing God*
C. S. Lewis, *Mere Christianity*
Annie Dillard, *Pilgrim at Tinker Creek*

Poetry
John Donne, Holy Sonnets and other "divine" poems
Gerard Manley Hopkins, any of his poetry
Wendell Berry, *Sabbaths*
John Milton, *Paradise Lost*
Dante Alighieri, *The Divine Comedy*
Fiction
C. S. Lewis, *Out of the Silent Planet, Perelandra* and *That Hideous Strength*
Frederick Buechner, *Godric*
Shusaku Endo, *The Silence* and *The Samurai*
Flannery O'Connor, "A Good Man Is Hard to Find"
Saul Bellow, *Mr. Sammler's Planet*
Garrison Kiellor, *Lake Woebegone Days*

Deism

Nonfiction
Albert Einstein, *Ideas and Opinions*
Poetry
Alexander Pope, *Essay on Man*
Fiction
Robert Pirsig, *Zen and the Art of Motorcycle Maintenance*

Naturalism

Nonfiction
Carl Sagan, *The Cosmos*
B. F. Skinner, *Beyond Freedom and Dignity*
J. Bronowski, *The Ascent of Man*
Kenneth Clark, *Civilization*
Loren Eisley, *The Unexpected Universe*
Poetry
Thomas Hardy, any of his poetry
Wallace Stevens, any of his poetry
Fiction
John Steinbeck, "Flight"
Thomas Hardy, *The Return of the Native* and
    Tess of the d'Urbervilles

Ernest Hemingway, *The Sun Also Rises*
B. F. Skinner, *Walden Two*
Stanislaw Lem, *The Cyberiad* and *The Futurological Congress*

Nihilism

Nonfiction
Helmut Thielicke, *Nihilism*
Friedrich Nietzsche, *Gay Science* and other writings in
    The Portable Nietzsche
Poetry
Stephen Crane, any of his poetry
Fiction
Joseph Heller, *Catch-22*
Franz Kafka, *The Trial* and *Parables and Paradoxes*
Samuel Beckett, *Waiting for Godot* and *Endgame*
Kurt Vonnegut, Jr., *Cat's Cradle*
Douglas Adams, *Hitch-hiker's Guide to the Galaxy* and its sequels

Existentialism: Atheistic

Nonfiction
Jean Paul Sartre, "Existentialism"
Albert Camus, *The Myth of Sisyphus* and *The Rebel*
Fiction
Albert Camus, *The Stranger* and *The Plague*
Jean Paul Sartre, *Nausea*
Friedrich Durrenmatt, "The Tunnel"

Existentialism: Theistic

Nonfiction
Søren Kierkegaard, *Fear and Trembling* and *Sickness unto Death*
Martin Buber, *I and Thou*
Fiction
Fyodor Dostoyevsky, *Underground Man* and
    The Brothers Karamazov

Eastern Pantheistic Monism

Nonfiction
The Upanishads, esp, as translated by Juan Mascaro and
    published by Penguin

Christmas Humphreys, *Buddhism*
K. M. Sen, *Hinduism*
Poetry
The Bhagavad-Gita
Gary Snyder, *Turtle Island* and *Axe Handles*
Allen Ginsberg, much of his poetry
Fiction
Hermann Hesse, *Siddhartha*
Philip K. Dick, *The Man in the High Castle*

New Consciousness

Nonfiction
Aldous Huxley, *Doors of Perception* and *Heaven and Hell*
Carlos Castaneda, *The Teachings of Don Juan* and its sequels
John Lilly, *Center of the Cyclone*
Shirley MacLaine, *Dancing in the Light*
Lewis Thomas, *The Lives of a Cell*
Poetry
Leonard Cohen, "Susanne Takes You Down"
Richard Brautigan, any of his poetry
Robert Bly, *News of the Universe*
Fiction
Richard Brautigan, *Troutfishing in America* and
  In Watermelon Sugar
Aldous Huxley, *Island*
Arthur Clarke, *2001* and *Childhood's End*

Step 1. Read through *The Universe Next Door* to get an overview
of Christian theism, deism, naturalism, nihilism, atheistic existentialism, theistic existentialism, Eastern pantheistic monism
and the new consciousness.

Step 2. Re-read chapter two of *The Universe Next Door* (on
Christian theism) and then one or two selected works from that
section of the chart, for example, John Stott's *Basic Christianity*
and C. S. Lewis's *Out of the Silent Planet*. Note the aspects of
Christian theism represented by those works; you will find, for
example, that various authors have different ways of expressing
similar concepts and, of course, that some of these differences

reflect more than verbal disagreements. Christian theism, like any world view, has a multitude of colors and shades.

Next, re-read chapter three of *The Universe Next Door* (on deism). There are not many obvious contempory examples of deistic writing. If you find *Zen and the Art of Motorcycle Maintenance* uninteresting or too "philosophic" for your taste, don't stop the plan; simply move on to naturalism.

Naturalism, the next world view, has been the dominant one in the Western world for the last two centuries. After re-reading chapter four of *The Universe Next Door,* read two or three selections from the naturalism section. I would especially suggest Carl Sagan's *The Cosmos,* John Steinbeck's "Flight" and Thomas Hardy's *Return of the Native.*

Take this same approach through the remaining world views, not trying to read every work in each section before moving on to the next.

Step 3. Read Francis Schaeffer's *How Should We Then Live?* to get a broad survey of Western intellectual history from a Christian perspective.

Step 4. Work your way again through the sequence of world views reading one or more further representative works from each section.

Step 5. Read Walsh and Middleton's *Transforming Vision,* a more detailed look at the Christian world view.

Step 6. Finish reading the remaining works on the list. Then begin to let your reading interests and what you have learned about other books and authors guide you into your own plan for a continued balanced diet of reading.

You are now on your own. You should be able to read virtually any work and find its place in the scheme of intellectual history and contemporary world views. More important you should also be growing intellectually, learning not only the world views of others but becoming able to understand your own, knowing why you hold it and why you think it true.

Selecting Periodicals
As I suggested in chapter six you will want to punctuate your

reading with periodicals. The following publications are the ones which over the past twenty years I have found to be most valuable. (Some, of course, have originated much more recently). The order here is from general to specific, the last five being magazines from a specifically Christian editorial perspective but a general topical scope.

Time (weekly), despite its frequent glib style and pugnacious arrogance, notes events and trends of immediate and long-range significance. Specific sections are devoted to world and national politics, the economy, energy, medicine, art, books, theater, and cinema. Some readers will prefer the style of *Newsweek* which parallels *Time* in topics covered. Both magazines frequently examine in some depth contemporary trends such as the occult, the new consciousness, violence in the streets, the energy crisis. These essays will lead the reader into other more extensive treatments in books and other publications.

Commentary (monthly) is an "intellectual" periodical with a generally liberal Jewish perspective, which comes out looking conservative by today's standards. The essays are often brilliant critiques of contemporary trends, and they are written with a sense of where history has been as well as where it is likely to go. The book reviews themselves are often penetrating essays.

The Atlantic and *Harper's* (both monthly) publish fiction, poetry and well-conceived essays on a variety of general topics of cultural interest. Both carry useful book reviews.

The Chronicle of Higher Education (weekly newspaper) announces and critiques developments in college and university education. Books of interest to the academic community are reviewed in depth; the essays on the final page, usually by influential teachers or administrators, display some of today's best thinking about the problems, goals and aspirations in higher education.

New York Times Book Review (weekly), reviewing a broad range of books—fiction, nonfiction, poetry—on the broadest range of topics, provides a helpful guide to what's worth reading. Some may prefer *The New York Times Review of Books* (biweekly).

Scientific American (monthly), as I have already mentioned, is unparalled in its field. With articles written by scientists who are closely associated with the research discussed, with editing that assures this writing will be eminently readable, and with clear and well-executed illustrations, charts and diagrams, *Scientific American* examines the cutting edge of scientific advance and comments on its human significance. The book reviews are also a valuable guide to more extensive treatments.

Christianity Today (fortnightly) for me is the most helpful Christian periodical. It carries news not only of events in Christendom but events in the larger culture which impinge on Christian life and thought. The essays by noted professional and academic writers are, for better or for worse, the best that is now being thought and said on a general theological and semi-academic level by Christians of an evangelical persuasion from all denominations. Books from a wide variety of viewpoints—liberal to conservative—are reviewed.

Eternity (monthly), an evangelical Christian magazine, has a less academically oriented reader in mind. Nonetheless, its articles and book reviews on all manner of topics of interest to contemporary Christians are often more penetrating than those in *Christianity Today.*

The Christian Century (weekly), a periodical of generally liberal stamp, carries articles by authors widely divergent in viewpoint. Books reviewed also range widely in content and point of view; the reviews are often incisive and insightful.

The Reformed Journal (monthly), bearing the editorial perspective of Calvinistic Christian thinking, is for those who wish to go a step deeper than the above journals. The authors are often the same, but here the editor has granted them the freedom to elaborate not only in the major essays but in the book reviews as well.

That is my list now. As time passes, it will change. Others will have different lists. Yours will be unique to you. It will include your specialty magazines. One of my daughters reads Spanish-language magazines, the other, *Creative Classrooms.* One of my sons has a subscription to *Keyboard Classics,* the other reads *Handyman.* I read *Free Inquiry.* The important matter is to get as broad a base for specialized reading as you can and then to do all your reading consciously from the standpoint of a developing world view of your own.

Notes & Index

Notes

Chapter 1
[1]Alvin Toffler, *Future Shock* (New York: Bantam, 1971), p. 155.
[2]Ibid., pp. 336-37.
[3]E. F. Schumacher, *Small Is Beautiful: Economics As If People Mattered* (New York: Harper and Row, 1975), p. 82.
[4]Kenneth B. Clark, "The Era of Psychotechnology," *Intellectual Digest,* Feb. 1972, p. 51.
[5]Ibid., p. 52.
[6]Samuel Taylor Coleridge, *Biographia Literaria,* XV, 4.
[7]For example, T. Norton Sterrett, *How to Understand Your Bible,* rev. ed. (Downers Grove: InterVarsity Press, 1974); R. C. Sproul, *Knowing Scripture* (Downers Grove: InterVarsity Press, 1977); and John R. W. Stott, *Understanding the Bible* (Glendale: Regal, 1972).

Chapter 2
[1]This essay appeared in the "Point of View" section on the back page of *The Chronicle of Higher Education,* February 9, 1976, p. 32. It is reprinted by permission from the publisher.

[2]Clark, p. 50.

[3]Woody Allen, "The UFO Menace," *Eastern Airlines Review,* Oct. 1977, p. 30.

[4]See, for example, Francis A. Schaeffer, *He Is There and He Is Not Silent* (Wheaton: Tyndale House, 1972), p. 43.

Chapter 3

[1]Literary purists will note that I am not using the best text for this poem, that is, the one to be found in Thomas H. Johnson, *The Complete Poems of Emily Dickinson* (Boston: Little, Brown and Company, 1960), p. 162. That is because it is the present text which I remember, having learned the poem long before the better text was published.

[2]W. H. Gardner and N. H. MacKenzie, eds., *The Poems of Gerard Manley Hopkins,* 4th ed. (London: Oxford University Press, 1967), p. 70.

[3]John Ciardi, *How Does a Poem Mean?* (Boston: Houghton Mifflin, 1959).

[4]Nathan A. Scott, Jr., "The Collaboration of Vision in the Poetic Act: The Religious Dimension," in *Literature and Belief,* ed. M. H. Abrams (New York: Columbia University Press, 1958), p. 112.

[5]Karl Beckson and Arthur Ganz, *A Reader's Guide to Literary Terms* (New York: Noonday Press, 1960), pp. 14, 22.

Chapter 4

[1]J. R. R. Tolkien, "On Fairy-Stories," in *The Tolkien Reader* (New York: Ballantine Books, 1966), p. 37.

[2]Tolkien, *The Tolkien Reader,* p. 85.

[3]Saul Bellow, *Mr. Sammler's Planet* (New York: Fawcett Publications, 1970), p. 215.

[4]Aldous Huxley, *Island* (New York: Bantam, 1963), p. 1.

[5]Ibid., p. 6.

[6]Aristotle, *Poetics,* in *Criticism: The Major Texts,* ed. Walter Jackson Bate, enlarged ed. (New York: Harcourt Brace Jovanovich, 1970), p. 23.

[7]Ibid.

[8]J. D. Salinger, *The Catcher in the Rye* (New York: Bantam, 1964), p. 1.

[9]Bellow, p. 7.

[10]Ibid.

[11]William Shakespeare, *As You Like It,* II, vii, 139-66.

[12]Robert Beum and James W. Sire, eds., *Papers on Literature: Models and Methods* (New York: Holt, Rinehart and Winston, 1970), p. 19.

[13]Beckson and Ganz, p. 6.

[14]Bellow, p. 11.

[15]Kurt Vonnegut, Jr., *Cat's Cradle* (New York: Dell, 1970), p. 19.

[16]See F. Scott Fitzgerald, *The Great Gatsby* (New York: Charles Scribner's Sons, 1953), pp. 23-26, 160.

[17]William Faulkner, "Barn Burning," in *Short Story Masterpieces,* ed. Robert Penn Warren and Albert Erskine (New York: Dell, 1954), pp. 162, 164, 166-67, 178, 180.

[18]The reference here may be to Sophocles' *Antigone,* 11. 583 ff., according to H. L. Brett, *Poems of Faith and Doubt: The Victorian Age* (London: Edward Arnold, 1965), p. 49.

[19]Ernest Hemingway, "Soldier's Home" in *Short Story Masterpieces,* pp. 213-14.

[20]Faulkner, p. 162.

Chapter 5

[1]Douglas Bush, "Literary History and Literary Criticism," in *Literary History and Literary Criticism: Acta of the Ninth Congress International Federation for Modern Languages Held at New York University, August 25 to 31, 1963,* ed. Leon Edel, Kenneth McKee and W. M. Gibson (New York: New York University, 1964) as reprinted in Bate, p. 699.

[2]Hopkins, pp. 99-100.

[3]Bush in Bate, p. 703.

[4]Scott, p. 112.

[5]Albert Camus, *L'Été,* quoted in John Cruickshank, *Albert Camus and the Literature of Revolt* (New York: Oxford University Press, 1960), p. 3.

[6]I have written in more detail about the connections between *The Plague* and existential philosophy in *The Universe Next Door* (Downers Grove: InterVarsity Press, 1976), pp. 108-12.

[7]Graham Hough, *A Preface to "The Faerie Queene"* (New York: W. W. Norton, 1962), p. 10.

[8]E. M. W. Tillyard, *The Elizabethan World Picture* (New York: Random House, 1943).

[9]C. S. Lewis, *The Discarded Image* (Cambridge: Cambridge University Press, 1964).

[10]Basil Willey, *The Seventeenth Century Background* (Garden City: Doubleday Anchor, 1955).

[11]H. G. Rosedale, "Milton: His Religion and Polemics, Ecclesiastical As Well As Theological," in *Milton Memorial Lectures,* ed. Percy W. Ames (London: Oxford University Press, 1909), pp. 178-86.

[12]John Milton, *Complete Poems and Major Prose,* ed. Merritt Y. Hughes (New York: Odyssey Press, 1957), pp. 900-02.

[13]Ronald Enroth, *Youth, Brainwashing and the Extremist Cults* (Grand Rapids, Mich.: Zondervan, 1977), p. 173. Enroth continues: "An incident related by an ex-member of the Children of God illustrates the mechanism of renunciation. In this case it involves a best-selling paperback book widely read in the youth subculture. 'One day I just happened to ask one of the brothers if he had ever read the book *Zen and the Art of Motorcycle Maintenance.* He asked, "What?" So I repeated my-

self, and he could not believe that I had said that. He asked, "Was it written by Mo [Moses David, leader of the Children of God]?" I said, "No." It completely astounded him that I had even thought to say such a thing. I really thought it was a good book. In fact, at the time I almost thought that it helped lead me to the Children of God. For the next half-hour he recited Bible verses to me about people who are not spiritually attuned with God. I was rebuked for mentioning the book' " (p. 173).

[14]In *The Universe Next Door,* pp. 20-42, I have presented Christian theism (the biblical world view) in more detail than this present study allows.

Chapter 6

[1]John Alexander, *Managing Our Work,* rev. ed. (Downers Grove: Inter-Varsity Press, 1975); and Ted W. Engstrom and Alex MacKenzie, *Managing Your Time* (Grand Rapids, Mich.: Zondervan, 1968).

[2]John White, *The Fight* (Downers Grove: InterVarsity Press, 1976), pp. 153-77.

[3]Paul E. Little, *Affirming the Will of God* (Downers Grove: InterVarsity Press, 1967).

[4]Charles E. Hummel, *Tyranny of the Urgent* (Downers Grove: Inter-Varsity Press, 1967).

[5]Charles W. Eliot, ed., "The Editor's Introduction," in *The Harvard Classics,* L (New York: P. F. Collier and Son, 1910), 3.

[6]*British Literature: From Beowulf to Sheridan,* ed. Hazelton Spencer, and *British Literature: From Blake to the Present Day,* eds. Hazelton Spencer, Walter E. Houghton and Herbert Barrows, 2nd ed. (Boston: D. C. Heath, 1963).

[7]E. M. Forster, "The Celestial Omnibus" in *The Art of Fiction,* ed. R. F. Dietrich and Roger Sundell (New York: Holt, Rinehart and Winston, 1967), p. 35.

[8]Ibid.

[9]Ibid., p. 46.

[10]Ibid.

[11]Ibid.

Index

Other Books in Shaw's **WHEATON LITERARY SERIES:**

Available from your local bookstore or from Harold Shaw Publishers, Box 567, Wheaton, IL 60189, 1-800-SHAWPUB